WARREN EVANS

VIRGINIA:
THE WESTERN
HIGHLANDS

Publishers:

EVANS GUIDES
P.O. Box 489
Waynesboro, Virginia 22980

RECOMMENDED
CHINA — THE RETURN OF MARCO POLO

Printed in the United States of America
Charles F. McClung, Printers, Inc.
Waynesboro, Virginia, U.S.A.

TABLE OF CONTENTS

Table of Contents (continued)

Catch The Rising Star.

Piedmont, the Up-And-Coming Airline, is now America's fastest-growing airline as well.

Since 1978, we've doubled the number of miles we fly. We've doubled the number of passengers we carry. We've even tripled our fleet of aircraft.

You can see why our star is rising. So catch our act for a truly outstanding performance.

✈ PIEDMONT

— *George Beetham*

Deer in Shenandoah National Park

PREFACE

For more than 30 years we have been laboring in the vineyard of tourism in one form or another. We have worked for a leading international airline in one of the nation's leading metropolises. We have operated a travel agency in which we have exported people to all parts of the world. We have visited a great majority of the world's magnificent destinations. Finally, we have written extensively on travel. Yet, something was still lacking.

We looked out our window one day and realized that living in the Shenandoah Valley for more than 25 years has been a privilege that we never fully appreciated. Our mission, professionally, had been to export people therefrom. At the same time in our own travels we continued to search for something quite unknown. In truth, we were seeking a touristic paradise. It was not until the very day that we looked out our own window that we realized that it was in our own backyard.

Western Virginia has no peer when it comes to furnishing all the ideal ingredients that build the package sought by discerning tourists. Let us reflect, for a moment, on the reasons why people travel. Many of us travel for pleasure served in a package of comfort. We demand that this be provided by courteous and well informed individuals. The traveler expects to pay a reasonable amount for services rendered. Today's tourist, because of the high cost of living, must be assured that when the vacation is over, there will be sufficient funds on hand to pay for the day to day existence that he faces.

When we travel we often attempt to satisfy our creature needs. We want good food and good lodgings. Cost must conform to pocketbook. Today's discerning traveler expects to be provided with service seasoned with cordiality, courtesy, and consideration. This service must be rendered with efficiency, if this is to have any meaning.

Today's tourist is vitally concerned with the problems surrounding transportation and logistics. We must have reasonable and simple access to the area that we visit. Of equal importance to the traveler is the ability to move within the area of visitation with a minimum of effort. The days of Lewis and Clark are not for the modern traveler. (Incidentally, these two adventurers commenced their travels from here.) Consideration must also be given to the cost of travel, if any vacation plan is to be complete.

Gone are the days when certain areas of the country were isolated from the mainstream. Here we have a region that is very much like an island of tranquility in an ocean of mass transited confusion. Interstates carry motorists to and from here with simplicity. Once here the visitor can take quiet country roads to a world of yesteryear's basic values. This is a region of individuals living together as opposed to individuals coping with the parameters of a high density population center. Here it is a slower and more relaxed pace. More time is available to concentrate and reflect on the real values that often escape us during the course of a day.

Campers have a special appreciation for the outdoors unfettered by the trappings that man makes to relieve the efforts connected with the "hard life." Here the outdoorsman can see the virgin forests as his bedroom. Here he can relive the past and at the same time enjoy the present without the pollution of the smokestack. It is a wonderful opportunity to meditate and contemplate. Something that few of us find the time to do in the course of a day. Here is the opportunity for the reshaping of future lives. Time for an accounting and an evaluation. If nothing else, here is the opportunity to marvel on the natural wonders that we never find in the smog filled landscape of the "other world."

The day to day existence causes many of us to forget that God never really intended for our planet to be wall to wall concrete. Had this been the plan, you can figure that we would now have an eight day week. The extra day would have been used for the construction of skyscrapers, city transit systems, and row housing.

It is not necessary to be a camper or outdoorsman to fully appreciate the natural wonders that abound. Surely the motorist can sit back as he drives through the majestic mountains and views the white water cascades that interrupt the peaceful flow of the clear mountain stream. There is time to pull off to the side of the road. Here we can do whatever contemplating or reflecting that our outdoor "cousin" does. No sleeping under the proverbial ceiling of stars for us. We can view the same stars from the front porch of our motel room. Not all of us are disposed for the active "thing." We are the ones that expect to have our creature comforts catered to, if our vacation is to be considered a grade "A" success. We are the viewers, not the doers. We prefer combining the view with the modern hotel and the ambience of the fine restaurant.

We appreciate the magnificent scenery that unfolds in front of us. We just want to take it in without physical exertion. We enjoy mountain ranges — but we do not want to go back to the old days when our cars had to navigate hairpin curves. We don't relish the old time steep ascents that caused radiators to overheat. Relaxed travel means good highways with unobstructed scenery. Our touristic paradise must be easy to enjoy.

The physical attractions of a region are very important in the selection of a God given paradise. Caves, caverns, lakes, natural bridges and other geological rock formations are the extras that we should search for in our travels.

Our experience in tourism points out the important role that host people must play, if a vacation is to be successful. The host's language should be readily understoood by the tourist. The culture should be diversified with a background somewhat different from what we see each day. The local cuisine should be tasty, digestible, and agreeable to the taste. We don't mind experimenting from time to time with foods different from our normal fare. But the truth of the matter is, that we yearn for dining not too unlike what we have always tasted in our homes.

There is one truth in tourism that is self evident — tourists love to buy. In our travels it is not uncommon for us to see people commencing their trips with a single bag. Yet upon return, they are like camels as they struggle with boxes, bags, and countless other items past the ever eager customs inspector.

Some of us enjoy browsing over antiques while there are others of us that prefer the discount emporiums. Shopping plays an important role in the world of travel. Shopping and traveling is nothing new. Let none of us forget, that Marco Polo purchased spaghetti in China, thereby converting the Italians into the pasta eaters that they are today. Ferdinand and Isabella employed Captain Columbus to find new lands so that he could bring back new spices to Spain. So, why should it not be reasonable for tourists to buy up the local offerings to bring back to their homes at journey's end?

By way of summation, we would say that we look for many things when we travel for pleasure. We look for romance — for comfort —convenience — nature — luxury — peace — contentment. We like to wander back into history and learn about the evolution of an area. We visualize ourselves transported to an earlier time. There are many objectives and many avenues to our varied goals.

This book contains information on many subjects of interest for many localities. You will read about sightseeing possibilities, shopping opportunities, festivals, sports, academic institutions, cultural possibilities, fishing, hunting, camping. The list is endless — we talk about transportation and logistics. Boiling it down, we have attempted to assemble every bit of encyclopedic information in an organized fashion to make a visit to western Virginia rewarding and enjoyable.

Western Virginia responds to the objectives of millions of the world's inhabitants. People from foreign lands know of our New York City, Los Angeles, Las Vegas, Washington, D.C., and Walt Disney World. Yet, when they pass through the Shenandoah Valley and wander through some of the more remote parts of southwest Virginia, their eyes open in amazement. Their amazement continues when they see the home of Thomas Jefferson and some of his fellow patriots.

First time travelers to western Virginia leave with a feeling of combined satisfaction and accomplishment. It has been a very rewarding experience to traverse a region of a single state that combines so very much diversification. Physical attractions coupled with an historical atmosphere served by a hospitable people. All of it served at a very reasonable price in a backdrop of contemporary timeliness.

It is interesting to note, that many native Americans learn about this touristic destination by sheer accident. It is while enroute from the colder northern climates to the warmer sub-tropical Floridian points that many a traveler has received his first taste of this truly enchanting area. It is from this brief tasting that an almost insatiable appetite arises, commanding the traveler to return over and over again for the purpose of extended visits. It is also of interest to note that professionals, retirees, and foreign sheiks have invested countless millions in property for either investment or residence in this paradisical area.

Prices are considerably lower than most other places in the country. Rewarding the tourist are countless places to explore, view, or shop.

The area is conservative yet very cosmopolitan. There is a blend of long time descendants of original settlers with recently relocated families. These natives find a source of employment with industries that expanded here from other parts of the country. Things are old and things are new. The work ethic is strongly expounded upon at an early age in the child's education. There is a strong spiritual backdrop in the local heritage. Educationally, the residents are above the national median.

The net results come in the form of fair dealings courteously administered by an honest populace. It appears to be a recall to "the good old days." It is a refreshing respite from the day to day jungle that so many of us have to survive in each day of our working life.

ABOUT THE BOOK

It is essential that the reader understand what this book attempts to do and the format that it will follow.

We have broken the target area into five regions. This has been done for convenience of both writer and reader. In truth, it serves no other purpose. The reader should regard this book as a tool or device, it should not be considered a "bible." We feel that this is the very first attempt to come up with a concise impartial book covering this total region. The editors, unlike many guidebook writers, have refrained from rating lodgings and dining facilities. We honestly feel that to do so would set ourselves up as pontificators of the highest degree. We have found, over the years, that we have personally enjoyed properties that guidebook writers have assigned uncomplimentary ratings.

Conversely, we have become nauseated at some highly touted inns. It is our considered belief that today's modern traveler is sufficiently versed and capable enough to seek out the best for his individual needs one way or the other.

We would point out that this book contains advertising. Our first reaction to the idea of including advertising was negative. Then on further reflection, we became excited about the prospects of including this truly American way of doing business. We believe that the reader will agree that this is a very ambitious undertaking. Our editors have attempted to secure from countless sources within the target area, timely information and other materials pertaining to their spheres of interest. It is to be borne in mind that this is a region of immense proportions. It is very diverse and contains so much of interest and detail. Hundreds of pounds of materials have been sifted through. Presentation of the final book with taste, care, and thoroughness is an objective of high priority.

We want outstanding graphics, beautiful pictures, and necessary maps. All of this is necessary, if this is to have any practical value for the user. A book of this magnitude must truly do justice to the beautiful locale that it attempts to depict. As producers of this, we must be cost conscious. This is especially important if it is to be purchased. Surely it would be inconsistent with the conservative nature of the locals, if we produce a guidebook beyond the means of the visitor. It is hoped that this book will be read by many people. It can not be done if the cost becomes prohibitive. Television, newspaper, radio, and magazine have found it necessary to rely upon advertising, if they are to market their product. We too, find it necessary to subsidize and underwrite the production through advertising.

Now, let us discuss the parameters that are being observed. Editorial content has been written with total objectivity. Each and every advertiser understands that the editorial content has been written based on merit and merit alone. Bathing suits are for getting wet —and towels are for getting dry. So shall it be with this book — the writer tells his story while the advertiser tells his.

There will be specially written articles by guest writers "kicking off" the various "regions." This will be followed by a treatment of certain specially selected communities within the region. The book's advertising will be blended with the written copy and will in most cases be found on the same pages as the communities that they help make up.

We sincerely believe that the ads will serve two purposes. Subsidizing the high cost of production was very necessary, if we were to make this book available at a very reasonable cost to the consumer. Secondly, the ad copy will provide the reader with definitive information on the subject of the ad.

Strict guidelines were established insofar as our advertising policy was concerned. Solicitation has been restricted to firms of good reputation. It is our hope that their offerings and their quality conforms to the spirit that the writers of this book hope to have established. We honestly believe that the advertising in this book will serve a positive need for the reader. The advertiser has been able to tell the story of his service to the reader.

Our readers have plenty of everyday practice in evaluating advertising in their daily lives. It is reasonable to assume that the reader will continue to make these same valued evaluations. Advertisers that tell their story convincingly will undoubtedly back up their ads with fact. We have faith in the integrity of the distributor of tourist services in western Virginia. We confidently present them on these pages for your ultimate consideration.

Our general format includes 17 specific classifications. These categories have been combined. We will review lodgings and dining in what we choose to call "laundry list" fashion. We shall attempt to give you address and phone number for each in that category. We have not included all of the possibilities. The reader will find that in this the first edition, we are relying upon information supplied by numerous sources. We shall attempt in subsequent editions to expand.

It is the considered belief of the editors that western Virginia is one of the best travel buys on the world market today. Most of the editors involved in this work have migrated here from other parts of the nation. We mention this by way of pointing out the objectivity of opinion. Those of us involved with this work truly believe that this is a pretty wonderful place to live and work. We sincerely subscribe to the statement, that it's a good place to live as well as visit. You are invited to use this book healthfully, happily as you travel the by-ways of western Virginia. You all hurry back.

— Warren Evans

THANK YOU! THANK YOU!

At the outset, this undertaking was commenced with the attitude that it would be simply a matter of good organization, management as well as writing. Little did we realize, at that time, that this book, if it was to materialize, would only result as the product of teamwork.

We look back to the beginning days and think of Dulaney Smith; she was responsible for getting the project started. Thanks to her enthusiasm and unbounded energy the program got off the ground.

We became indebted, at the outset, to Laverne Deusebio and Martha Steger of the Virginia Division of Tourism. Their tangible advice got this project off the drawing board. Proudly, we admit that some materials used in this book came from The Virginia Division of Tourism.

Before departing the world of state government, we must doff our hat to Dr. Charles Sydnor, a staff member of great importance to his Excellency, Charles Robb, Governor of Virginia. His tangible help along with that of the Governor, himself, adds so much to the credibility of this publication.

On the opposite side of the political coin, we are equally indebted to Eric Peterson, a key legislative aide for John Warner, the senior United States Senator from the Commonwealth of Virginia. So oft times we forget that great men can not operate at peak efficiency without the Eric Petersons and the Charles Sydnors of the world. We offer personal thanks to the Senator himself for his input into this book. We involved in tourism in this country owe a great personal debt to Senator Warner!

Next, we must offer thanks for the encouragement and practical guidance that we have received from Joe Grandstaff, Executive Director of the Shenandoah Valley Travel Association. As a true working professional in the vineyard of western Virginia tourism, his input has been vital to the success of this project.

None of this could have taken place without the help and contribution from the professional staffs of the more than 53 individual Chambers of Commerce within the "Target Area."

The assistance that we have received from the Department of Highways and Transportation has been so important to all of us involved with the publication. Without their tireless accomplishments very few of us would have the opportunity to visit, in depth, this very beautiful and historic area. We also are greatly indebted, as highway users, for the publication and free distribution of their outstanding map, Virginia Official State Highway and Transportation Map. We certainly suggest that motorists reading this book avail themselves of a copy.

There are so many persons that have played an important role in the development of this publication. We must thank our very good friend, Jim Webster, of Associated Advertising, for the very practical advice that he has rendered. We can not forget our very good friends of Charles McClung, Printers, that have been so patient and professional in making this book the reality that it is.

Never can we forget our own special friends at Shenandoah Microcomputer Services, Wayt Gibbs and Frank Walters. This very strange era that we think of as the day of the microcomputer has created great need for the very important Wayts and Franks. Without them, surely this writer would be at a complete loss to operate such sophisticated machinery.

We must sincerely thank Ann Perkins, who in spite of severe pain and other debilitating discomforts resultant from serious surgery, devoted so many hours to this project. Her input of ideas and patience in working with us will always be remembered.

Unquestionably, the one that we owe the greatest measure of thanks is Kay, our wife. She has been exceedingly supportive of our efforts. She has encouraged us to continue, when at times, we became discouraged. She turned her cheek the other way when we became short and cantankerous as the result of "artistic temperament." She has been tolerant of the Saturdays, Sundays, holidays, and late hours, that we have kept during this work. We thank her for the very constructive suggestions that she has given to this book. We also thank her for bringing us, so many years ago, to western Virginia, her home and now that of this writer.

When we think of people to thank, we are also grateful to Louis Spilman, one of the best travel writers that we have ever read. From him we have matured in the ability to portray persons and places to others. We are also deeply grateful to have had the privilege of knowing this great man these many years.

To our own Mother, Annette, we must ever be mindful of the sacrifices that she made to provide us with the education that the creation of a tome such as this required.

There are so many others that we should recall at this time. Prayerfully, we hope that those that we have omitted will forgive our lapse of memory. Yet as important as each person and agency is that we have named, none is more important than those that we remember in the final paragraph.

All thanks must go to the Commonwealth of Virginia with its scenery, resources, and its overwhelming and dramatic beauty. Her land and her ever friendly and hospitable people have made this project, for all of us involved, an enjoyable and educational experience that will never be forgotten. And last, but surely far from least, we must thank God for making it all possible.

— Warren Evans

COMMONWEALTH of VIRGINIA

Office of the Governor
Richmond 23219

Charles S. Robb
Governor

Welcome to Virginia!

I'm delighted to have this opportunity to add a personal word of greeting to all of you who will be traveling and enjoying the beautiful region of our Commonwealth that has been so well and thoroughly described for you in <u>Virginia-The Western Highlands.</u>

In the pages that follow, you will find a wealth of information that I am confident will be both informative and useful as a guide in helping you plan where to go and what to see.

The western part of our Commonwealth, that curves along the graceful arc running from Winchester, through the eastern slopes of the Blue Ridge, and down the Roanoke Valley to the Cumberland Gap in our great Southwest -- this western part of Virginia is an area extraordinarily rich in history, in diversity, and in beauty. It is, moreover, an area that has given much over the course of two centuries to the unique character of Virginia. The energetic, friendly Virginians you will meet everywhere throughout the western part of the Commonwealth reflect the qualities and the progressive spirit that have made the entire area so dynamic and attractive since it was first settled. It was from western Virginia that the hardy ancestors of Abraham Lincoln began a journey that was to end in Illinois and presidential greatness. And it was the original Virginians of the region who transformed the great barrier of the Appalachians into the original gateway to the Ohio and Mississippi valleys.

The western part of Virginia will give you much to sense and feel, both in the history of our Commonwealth and our nation. Thomas Jefferson thought and dreamed and wrote here. Stonewall Jackson revolutionized modern military history here. The greatness of George Marshall was formed in the education, the values, and the experience he drew from here. Woodrow Wilson carried throughout his life the qualities and the characteristics that had shaped the region in which he was born.

The most important qualities the western part of Virginia has to offer its visitors are the senses, the values and the natural wonders that have become the ingredients we, as Virginians, treasure most in our way of life -- our civility, our enthusiasm and love for the land that is ours, and our eagerness to share the wonders all around us with all those who become our guests.

In this region, you will find, as countless others have, that the people live in a spirit that looks upon our Commonwealth, as more than a state, more even than a way of life. You will find in those you meet the living belief that to be in Virginia is to come closest to the things that mean the most in life.

These Virginians live and work and play daily amidst impressions our guests take home as memories indelibly etched for a lifetime: mist receding in the dawn in the Shenandoah Valley; the soft, but stunning lines of deep green and brilliant blue at the juncture of earth and sky in the Cumberland Gap; the vivid memories of great actors and careers of world fame, begun on the stage of the Barter Theatre in Abingdon, the virtuoso performance of nature in the unrivaled autumnal splendor of the Blue Ridge; the stillness that even now embraces the fields of New Market on a spring afternoon; the timeless whisper of the James in its dialogue with us along it voyage to the sea; the awed silence of bare-legged school children gazing at Jefferson's tomb on the grounds at Monticello.

These are the unique qualities of this magnificent region of Virginia -- qualities that must be seen to be experienced, felt to be savored. They are among the greatest gifts we can offer our visitors; they are the priceless treasures we are eager to share with you as our guests.

I hope you might have the opportunity to see and experience all of these wonders, and the equally abundant attractions throughout western Virginia that can enrich your travels with a wealth of impressions, a fund of memories, we believe you will carry with you always.

We are delighted you have come to visit; we hope you have a wonderful time in our Commonwealth; and we look forward to having you return soon, and often, to the western part of Virginia.

Charles S. Robb
Governor

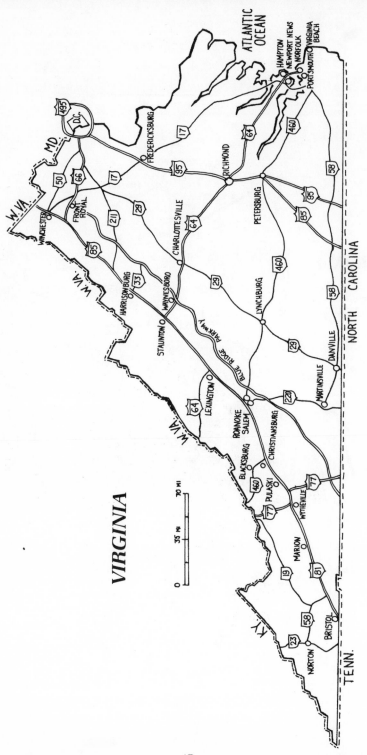

VIRGINIA

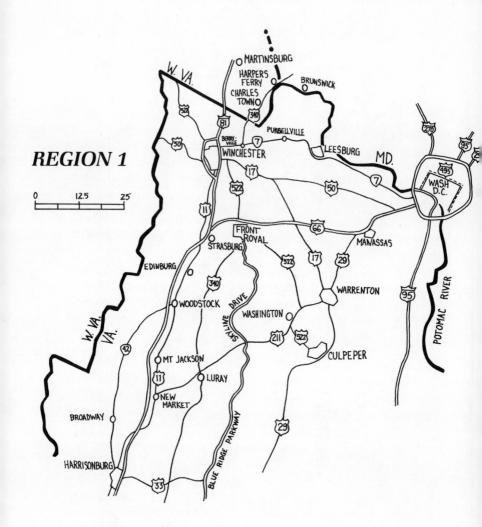

REGION 1

MARTINSBURG
HARPERS FERRY
CHARLES TOWN
BRUNSWICK
W. VA.
522
81
340
PURCELLVILLE
BERRY-VILLE
50
7
WINCHESTER
LEESBURG
MD.
17
522
50
7
11
66
WASH D.C.
495
270
95
FRONT ROYAL
STRASBURG
MANASSAS
EDINBURG
522
17
29
WOODSTOCK
340
WARRENTON
95
SKYLINE DRIVE
WASHINGTON
42
211
522
MT JACKSON
CULPEPER
11
LURAY
NEW MARKET
BLUE RIDGE PARKWAY
POTOMAC RIVER
BROADWAY
29
HARRISONBURG
33
W. VA.
VA.

0   12.5   25

Virginia — Gateway to America, Center of American History

by U.S. Senator John W. Warner

From the shores of the Atlantic to the peaks and caverns of the Blue Ridge, Virginia offers visitors a travel experience unequalled any place on earth.

Within a short distance, travelers can explore America's founding, its struggle to maturity, and its efforts to meet the challenges of the present and the future. In northern Virginia alone, the adventurous can traverse 200 years of history and be propelled well into the 21st century, all within 50 square miles.

Arriving by air at one of three major airports serving the Washington metropolitan area, coming by car via Interstate routes 66, 95 or 70, by Amtrak, or bus, vacationers quickly find Arlington or Alexandria an ideal base from which to explore the many attractions of the nation's capital; the homes, meeting places and business establishments of America's founding fathers; the Civil War battlefields at Manassas and Bull Run; and the laboratories and assembly lines of some of the world's high-technology leaders.

Whether one tours by car or by foot, the sense of historic importance is overwhelming, and with a little imagination, visitors can quickly place themselves in the midst of events past, present and future — reliving the making of America and anticipating its future.

For example, my home, the Atoka Farm near Middleburg, about 50 miles from Washington, D.C., was the campsite for one of the most interesting Confederate warriors, John Singleton Mosby. He was commander of Mosby's Raiders, a renegade fighting group which nearly succeeded in its efforts to defeat Union troops during the Civil War.

As I stand on the lawn in front of my farm home, I can picture Major Mosby huddled with his men around the campfire plotting the day's tactics. They will set a trap for Union soldiers at Manassas, just a half-day's journey by horse, then retreat at nightfall.

Further to the west lies the Shenandoah River and the Blue Ridge Mountains. Early pioneers relied on the Shenandoah as a commercial thoroughfare. The Blue Ridge Mountains were the gateway to the new frontier, the wilderness and the great unknown.

To the east of Atoka lies Dulles International Airport, a growing center for international commerce and one of a handful of landing ports for the highly advanced British/ French Concorde supersonic passenger jet.

But northern Virginia is not the only vantage point from which the traveler can sample the bounty of Virginia, past, present and future.

Richmond, the Commonwealth's capital, was also the capital of the Confederacy. Today, it is home for some of America's leading transportation companies, agricultural enterprises, and scientific endeavors.

From Richmond, visitors can easily travel to Charlottesville, home of the University of Virginia and Monticello, Thomas Jefferson's home stead. Travelers may also wish to explore the tobacco and peanut farms of south central Virginia, or take advantage of numerous other nearby scenic, historic or commercial attractions.

Further to the east is the Tidewater region of Virginia. The first settlers to the new world made their home at Jamestown. Colonial Williamsburg was the first capital of Virginia, and today is a living museum of those days gone by. Norfolk, Newport News, Portsmouth and Chesapeake are home to major shipbuilding activities and one of the U.S. Navy's largest ports. Here visitors can tour the latest naval technology, experiencing for themselves life on a huge aircraft carrier, frigate or naval destroyer.

The Tidewater region is also the home of Virginia's seafood industry. Restaurants throughout the area feature fresh oysters, crabs, lobster, bluefish and other delicacies of the Chesapeake Bay and the Atlantic Ocean.

But there's more to Virginia than its historic past, its coastline and its mountains. Virginia has a heartland too, filled with the richnesss of southern hospitality, of country living, and the folklore of farmers, coalminers, and laborers.

So, welcome to Virginia, gateway to America, center of America history.

Once you're here, you'll understand why all times are exciting times in Virginia.

BERRYVILLE AND CLARKE COUNTY

Lodgings: (703)

You are only 50 miles west of Washington, D.C. in distance; though in time, it is hundreds of years away. You are now in a particular corner of Virginia. Here, one is able to relive American history with the Colonial era. You will pass through the Revolution and live through the Civil War. In addition to your sojourn with history, you will have ample opportunity to view magnificent scenery. Why not take one of the ancient back roads along the banks of the Shenandoah River? What a wonderful opportunity to get away even further from that civilized 50 miles distance that separates you from the nation's capitol.

Lodgings: (703)
Blue Ridge Bed & Breakfast, 955-3955
L'Auberge Provencale, 837-1375
Farm Motel, 837-1692

Dining
The Lighthouse Restaurant
The Meeting Place Restaurant & Pub

Dining In White Post
L'Auberge Provencale (Reservations)
The Farm Restaurant & Motel

THE BERRYVILLE-CLARKE COUNTY Chamber of Commerce has printed a small folder that you will find most handy. Why not drop them a line at: P.O. Box 365, Berryville, VA 22611. They are located at 5 S. Church Street. There is a map on the centerfold with a legend of the various stops that you may want to make on your tour.

There are numerous buildings of interest in the area dating back to the 18th Century. As an example, we would mention Norwood which was built in 1778 and North Hill dating back to 1774. In addition, there is Fairfield built in 1770 for Warner Washington. It was regarded as one of the most beautiful of its time.

THE HOLY CROSS ABBEY AND MONASTERY is also located here. The Trappist monks, living under the Rule of St. Benedict, lead their contemplative lives in a spirit of total harmony. The monastery will, today, serve as a sanctuary of retreat for numerous individuals not associated with the Order. The site for the abbey was originally a home built in 1784 and named Cool Spring.

The yellow folder, published by the Chamber of Commerce, that we earlier referred to includes a code system that tells the passerby whether the property is open to the public or may be viewed by appointment. There is even a code telling the user whether viewing may be accomplished from the road.

One of the sights that is open to the public without restriction is the Blandy Experimental Farm. This is an arboretum owned by the University of Virginia that is open sunrise to sunset.

In the town of White Post (supposedly named after the white post that George Washington put into the ground to mark the direction of Lord Fairfax's home), is a very interesting business enterprise. We are talking about White Post Restorations. This firm dedicates its efforts to the restoration of antique cars. They are reputed to be one of the world's foremost leaders of antique classic car restoration —837-1140.

It is reasonable to search for antiques when you hit an area such as this. There are several dealers in Berryville. Before leaving this oft omitted section, we would point out that the population of Berryville will possibly run less than 2000. Nearby are the famed Byrd Orchards which were at one time the largest individually owned apple orchards in the world. We should not leave here without making mention that such memorable names as Admiral Richard Byrd and Senator Harry Byrd called this their home.

— Virginia Division of Tourism

Piedmont Point-to-Point Steeplechase, Upperville

CULPEPER

Lodgings: (703)
Holiday Inn, US 29, 825-1253
Econo Lodge, US 29/15, 825-5097
Sleepy Hollow Motel, US 29/15, 825-8396

Dining:
Country Cookin', Southgate Shopping Center, 825-6565
Fireside Restaurant, Holiday Inn, US 29, 825-1253
John's Family Pizza, Southgate Shopping Center, 825-5575
Kentucky Fried Chicken, 410 S. Main St., 825-2500
McDonald's, 100 James Madison Hwy, 825-5678
Pete's Pizza, Culpeper Shopping Center, 825-9111
Pizza Hut, 876 N. Main, 825-6550
Big T Family Restaurant, 29 N. Brandy Rd., 825-8722
Gayheart's (Fountain Service), 101 E. Davis, 825-3600
Wendy's, 872 N. Main
Hardee's, S. Main Street

History

The Town of Culpeper was first called Fairfax and was established in 1759. The name business is quite interesting. Catherine Culpeper, the daughter of Lord Thomas Culpeper, married Lord Fairfax VI hence the town was named after him. Some 10 years before this the county courthouse had been named Culpeper Courthouse. So, you guessed it — the name Fairfax never caught on — the town was destined to be known as Culpeper. Culpeper County was first settled in 1722 from a part of Orange County. Purists undoubtedly consider the year 1749 as the beginning date for the town. The U. S. Post Office designated the town as Culpeper Courthouse in 1795. In 1870 the General Assembly resolved the whole business of names by officially designating the town as Culpeper.

Students of early American history recall that George Washington was a surveyor. It is appropriate to point out at this time that at the age of 17, he was the first one to survey Culpeper County.

The Culpeper Minute Men were the first to respond to Patrick Henry's call to arms in 1775.

From local sources we learn that the town served as military headquarters for both sides during the Civil War. Intense fighting took place in the county during the war.

Sightseeing

Salubria, a Georgian home, dates back to 1743 and is the oldest brick house in the county. It is located eight miles out on Route 3. Tours are given by appointment.

BURGANDINE HOUSE — The oldest building in town dates back to around 1749. It was a tavern. Tours by appointment.

LITTLE FORK CHURCH — A restored colonial church built in 1776 and located near Rixeyville on Route 624.

ST. STEPHEN'S EPISCOPAL CHURCH at 115 North East Street was built in 1821.

MONUMENTS — Minute Men on Route 522 W.; Confederate in Fairview Cemetery on Route 522 West.

In addition to the above, there are several buildings of interest that are being utilized today — birthplace of General A. P. Hill is a downtown commercial building; Greenwood, an 18th Century home visited by Lafayette, is a private residence.

NATIONAL CEMETERY is also located here.

CULPEPER COUNTY COURTHOUSE at West & Davis Streets houses records dating back to 1749.

GERMANNA FORD — On Route 3 some 3.7 miles southeast of Lignum is the site of the original colony founded by Governor Alexander Spotswood and settled by German iron miners in 1714. Germanna Community College is located on part of the original land.

BATTLEFIELDS — Brandy Station — The largest cavalry battle in the western hemisphere was fought on Fleetwood Hill during the Civil War. Located outside of the Village of Brandy Station. Cedar Mountain — This civil War battle site is located six miles south of town on Route 15.

The local library has an interesting genealogical section on Virginia families as well as a good fine arts section.

CULPEPER CAVALRY MUSEUM located in the Chamber of Commerce building. It contains an outstanding display of Civil War items. Open during week days from 9 to 4. Admission is free.

VIRGINIA BAPTIST HOME — Situated on a beautiful 625 acre farm and located on Route 15 south of town.

RAPIDAN RIVER FARMS — Stated to be the largest and best equipped Morgan horse breeding farm in the country. The farm is located 15 miles east of town off Route 3 on Route 681. Visitors welcome.

ZEUSWYN FARM — Breeder of registered Angus on US 29 South.

FREEDOM STUDIES CENTER — Research and education in the field of national security. It is housed on an 825 acre estate near

Boston (US 522 NW). There are seminar, library, classroom, and publication facilities. The Center offers a full time Freedom Academy program.

FEDERAL RESERVE COMMUNICATIONS CENTER — This is a bunker-like facility carved into a hillside housing records and having sophisticated computer operations which handle communications for the entire Federal Reserve System. There are tours for selected groups when requested a week in advance.

MOUNTAIN RUN LAKE — Lakeside park with picnic, boating, and fishing.

HUNTING — Quail, deer, fox, turkey and doves.

Geography & Population
The county is primarily rural in nature. Its residents enjoy fresh water and clean air. The county is situated on terrain that ranges from level to rolling hills. It is situated on US 29, a four lane road that links Charlottesville with Washington, D.C. The county population is about 23,000 while the town runs around 7,000.

Transportation
Nearest air service would be from Charlottesville with other service from Dulles and National Airports in Northern Virginia. Trailways provides bus service and the Norfolk & Southern furnishes rail. Municipal airport six miles north of town serving small aircraft.

Climate
Four normal seasons with some snow in winter. Some days of 90 degree heat in summer. Annual precipitation runs about 40 inches.

Potpourri
Civil War was re-enacted during August, 1983 as part of Culpeper Pride Week. It was sponsored by the Culpeper Cavalry Museum and the Culpeper Chamber of Commerce. Re-enactment of the Battle of Cedar Mountain was done on August 21st — the first time it took place was on August 9, 1862. Viewers were able to see the "soldiers" set up battlefield conditions, tent camps and field kitchens. Spectators were even given a play by play of what was going to happen. Units came from as many as 10 states. The Battle of Cedar Mountain is expected to be renewed on a biennial basis — it will alternate with the Battle of Brandy Station. Further information can be secured from: Culpeper Cavalry Museum, 135 W. Davis Street, Culpeper, VA 22701.

FRONT ROYAL
Lodgings: (703)
Center City Motel, 416 S. Royal Ave., 635-4050
Constant Spring Inn, 413 S. Royal Ave., 635-7010
Cool Harbor Motel, 15 & Shenandoah Ave., 635-2191
Midtown Motel, 1122 N. Royal Ave., 635-2196
Pioneer Motel, 541 S. Royal Ave., 635-4784
Quality Inn, 522 By-Pass, 635-3161
Scottish Inn, 533 S. Royal Ave., 636-6168
Twi-Lite Motel, 53 W. 14th St., 635-4148
Twin Rivers Motel, 1800 Shenandoah Ave., 635-4101
Wayside Inn Since 1797, Middletown, 869-1797

Campgrounds: (703)
KOA-Three Springs Campground, Rt. 340 S. 635-2741
Gooney Creek Camp, Rt. 340 S. 635-4066

Restaurants: (703)
Belle Boyd, 643 S. Royal Ave., 636-6556
Constant Spring, 413 S. Royal Ave., 635-7010
Golden China Restaurant, 1423 Shenandoah, 636-9340
Hardee's, 8th & N. Royal, 636-6386
Howard Johnson's, 14th & Shenandoah, 635-3466
Kentucky Fried Chicken, 1204 N. Royal Ave., 635-7119
McDonald's, South Street, 935-9150
Melting Pot, 138 W. 14th St., 636-6146
My Father's Moustache, 106 S. Royal Ave., 635-3496
Pizza Hut, 22 W. 14th St., 635-4091
Quality Inn, 522 By-Pass, 635-3161
Tastee Freez Big Tee, Rt. 55 E, 635-2548
Wayside Inn, Middletown, 869-1797
Wendy's, 836 Commerce Ave., 636-6857
Golden Corral, 101 W. 14 Street, 636-2839
Royal Pizza, 109 S. Royal Ave., 636-2510
La Fiesta Mexican Restaurant, 916 John Marshall Hwy., 635-7348
Hamilton Restaurant, Woodstock, 459-4086
Pizza Hut, I-81, Ex. 72, 459-4502
Spring House Restaurant, I-81, Ex. 72, 459-4755

FRONT ROYAL & WARREN COUNTY
Visitors coming to the area for the first time shake their heads. So many times these first timers have been heard asking, "are we really in Virginia?"

"What, in truth, did you expect to find when you came here?" We would counter. "I don't really know. I guess maybe I was looking for plantations and magnolias."

"Are you disappointed?"

Cool Harbor
Motel

Betty & Chris Christensen
Hosts

15th & Shenandoah Avenue
Front Royal, Va. 22630

Telephone
(703) 635-2191

"Oh! No! It's really breathtaking beauty. We just didn't know that it would be this way."

Virginia is a very diversified state and also a very large one. There are mountains, rolling hills, urban sprawls, swamps, and ocean. There is history and there is today. There is beautiful scenery and there is super scenery. In truth, there are even spots that can't be considered better than so so. Yet, as a whole no state of the 50 can boast greater diversification of scenery, demography, culture, economics. The list goes on and on. We truly feel that this region of the state that you are entering and passing through is just about the most wonderful piece of real estate mile for mile any place in the world.

We have no axe to grind as we put together this collection of travel aids. We came here from many miles away. We chose to stay. Many others have done the same thing. Maybe you will be so inclined. But, even if you don't, it is well to mention that you are one of about 2,000,000 that will pass through here this year. Let us now tell you something about the area:

Some Formal Facts
Warren County's population is 21,035 of which Front Royal counts 11,151 according to the 1980 census. This registers a gain of more than 35% over 1970. They are projecting 34,300 for the total by 2000. These are revealing facts. They tell us that if we want to keep away from the urban hustle and bustle there is sure to be tranquility here until the beginning of the new millenium, at least.

The elevation here is 566 feet. They have a small private airport. The nearest commercial service is in Charlottesville. There is also the alternative of flying from either Dulles or National Airport to the north. Shenandoah Valley Airport in Weyers Cave might also work out, if you have business in Harrisonburg, Staunton, or Waynesboro.

The weather is moderate with four different seasons, not unlike the surrounding area. The climate is comparable to the surrounding area. There are some very hot days in summer and some very cold in winter. They do have snow but it is not excessive — a couple of snowfalls per year.

Front Royal is blessed with excellent highways in and out of town. The driver with plenty of time may use the Skyline Drive. It wends its way west through the Shenandoah National Park to Waynesboro. The distance is 105 miles. You can't rush — but, if you have the time it is worth the trip. During the season there are places to stop for snacks and gas along the route. You have access to the Drive from I-66, I-81, or I-64. US 340, US 211, and US 33 intersect.

In addition to the Skyline Drive, one can go to and from Front Royal by I-81, I-66, and US 340.

SHENANDOAH NATIONAL PARK — In other sections of the book we have given more detailed data on reservations for park facilities. ARA-Virginia Sky-Line Co., P.O. Box 727, Luray, VA 22835, should be addressed for reservations information at any of the lodges. Camping information can be secured from the National Park Service at Luray, VA.

FACT OR FABLE — The name Front Royal is said to have come about as the result of a close order drill situation during the French and Indian Wars. It is stated that a British drill master had trouble getting his commands across to his troops while they drilled on the town square. In the square grew a great oak tree — the Royal tree of England. The frustrated but innovative officer coined a new command on the spot: "Front the Royal Oak." This was given in order to get his troops properly lined up. In time the command was shortened to Front Royal.

Jackson's Valley Campaign started here. Front Royal was also the base of operations for the famed Mosby's Raider's.

What To See
We have already discussed the National Park in great detail elsewhere in this book. But, keep in mind that there are interesting

drives, hikes, and camping opportunities. Through adequate advanced planning, you might consider staying at one of the lodges and using it as a base for sightseeing and other activities.

MIDDLETOWN — Here is located the very quaint Wayside Inn which was established in 1797. You might choose to eat there or sleep there. About a block away is the Wayside Theater for professional entertainment.

THUNDERBIRD MUSEUM AND ARCHEOLOGICAL PARK There are artifacts here that date back to 9500 B.C. They were excavated at the Thunderbird site. Here is an opportunity to view exhibits in the museum that tell about man's history in the Shenandoah Valley. The Corral Site is an ongoing archeological excavation on the grounds of the Museum and Archeological Park. If you are there during the summer, you will be able to see the archeologists at work. It is fascinating to learn more about this 3000 year old site, first hand. You can ask questions and get answers. In addition, there are three miles of nature trails within the park. The museum includes an introductory slide show. Visitors will find an opportunity to even shop for locally produced crafts. The Archeological Park is made up of 86 acres along the South Fork of the Shenandoah River. Here is an opportunity to hike the trails and picnic in wooded areas so set aside.

The park is open from mid-March to mid-November. There is an admission charge. For further information: Thunderbird Museum & Archeological Park, Rt. 1, Box 432, Front Royal, VA 22630, 635-7337 or 635-3860.

DINOSAUR LAND — Between Winchester and Front Royal is this attraction replete with authentic reproductions of prehistoric life. Closed during January and February. Further information: Dinosaur Land, Rt. 1, Box 63A, White Post, VA 22663, 869-2222.

CONFEDERATE MUSEUM — Front Royal-95 Chester Street. There is a nominal charge for admission at this museum that is opened from April 15th until November 1st. During the balance of the year, they will accommodate through appointment. Included within the museum are relics and records of this divisive war. Also included are: arms, battleflags, uniforms, cavalry equipment, documents, pictures and memorabilia. For further information: 636-9068, 635-2692, 635-2478.

PASSION PLAY — If you can't wait for Oberammergau, why not consider the American version which is held in Strasburg's garden theater nightly except Monday at 8:30 PM from June to Labor Day. In the event there is rain, the performance is held at the Randolph-Macon Auditorium in Front Royal. The cast is made up of professionals and local talent. For additional information: 465-3688.

SKYLINE CAVERNS — Nature's handicraft is on display and should certainly be included in your program at one time or another. It is here that you will find anthodite formations. By the time you leave here, you will know about stalactites and stalagmites. Included is an underground stocked trout stream. Open year round. Further information: 635-4545.

SHENANDOAH VINEYARDS — Edinburg. Here is an opportunity to visit some vineyards — as a matter of fact, they are the first in the Shenandoah Valley. There are 15 acres here. For further information: 984-8699.

FESTIVAL OF THE LEAVES — This is usually a two day affair including varied festivities taking place in October.

Further information on the Front Royal area can be secured from the Chamber of Commerce, P.O. Box 568, Front Royal, VA 22630, 635-3185.

LEESBURG
Lodgings: (703)
Laurel Bridgade Inn, 20 W. Market St., 777-1010
Little Rock Motel, Rt. 4, Box 608, 777-3499
Sigwick Inn, 110 Clubhouse Dr., 471-9275
Weona Village Motel, Rt. 7, Box 141, 338-7000

Dining: (703)
Aiken Sizzling Steaks, 301 Fort Evans Rd., 777-7301
The Bailiwick, 26 Plaza St., 777-3340
Chez Jake, 268 E. Market St., 777-5253
China King, 5 S. King St., 777-9652
Green Tree, 15 S. King St., 777-7246
Hawaiian, 170-E Catactin Circle, 777-9444
Johnson's Charcoal Beef House, 203 E. Market St., 777-1116
King's Court Tavern, 2C W. Loudoun St., 777-7747
Laurel Brigade Inn, 20 W. Market St., 777-1010
Leesburg Restaurant, 9 S. King St. 777-3292
McDonald's, 157 E. Market St., 777-9600
Mighty Midget Kitchen, 117 E. Market St., 777-1496
Sigwick Dining Room, 1100 Clubhouse Dr., 777-1910
Uncle Abe's Pizza Parlor, 20 W. Loudoun St., 777-3222

MIDDLEBURG
Lodgings: (703)
Red Fox Tavern, Washington & Madison Streets, 687-6301
Little River Inn, Aldie, 327-6742
Welbourne, VA, 743/687-3201

Dining: (703)
Cafe Le Rat, 2 W. Marshall St., 687-6223
Coach Stop Restaurant, 28½ Washington St., 687-5515
Red Fox Tavern, 2 W. Washington St., 687-6800

LOUDOUN COUNTY
This stately and affluent county is approximately 25 miles northwest of Washington, D.C. Here we have an example of a tasteful blending of yesterday's gentility with today's advanced creativity. We pass mile after mile of well tended estates in the western part of the county. It is on the other side that we see modern buildings that house the forerunners for tomorrow's advanced high technology.

Loudoun County is the site for one of the world's most advanced and confusion free airports. Dulles Airport was built years ahead of its time. Travelers find adequate parking facilities and are treated to convenient terminal facilities that negate the need to be proficient at roller skating. The various airline counters and boarding gates are within convenient walking distance of each other. The architecture of the terminal building is striking and still today after years of use appears to be designed in the 21st Century. Yes, even this modern airport blends into the communal county scene.

Population for the county is about 60,000. There are four seasons here with moderate temperatures for each of the four. Precipitation will average 40 inches a year with approximately 24 inches of snowfall.

The area is properly served with highways going in all directions and of many varieties. There are the county roads and the larger and wider state roads which lead to the federal highways and interstates. This is either the last opportunity to enjoy a modicum of traffic sanity. People coming from the urban centers regard it as a transition to something better. You are well advised to study your map as you travel the county lest you find yourself on a highway to urban chaos.

The menu of schools of higher learning knows no boundaries. From here residents attend colleges and universities the world over. In the immediate radius of a hundred miles, there are schools that specialize in everything from computer programming to the sale of travel. All of these are in addition to the traditional academic institutions. The Loudoun Campus of Northern Virginia Community College is in close proximity as well as George Mason University. Additional colleges are located in Washington, D.C. and Maryland. Needless to say, students from this area also attend the various universities located in other parts of the state.

Finally, when we talk of the local economy we should hasten to point out that this can well be considered a bedroom community for Washington, D.C. Many people of the area hold positions with the federal government. There are many members of Congress and other high government officials that deign to call Loudoun County their home away from home.

What To See And Where
If you look back into the 1750's, you will be learning about the first days of Leesburg and the county. Certainly, it is not our purpose to discuss the history of the county. There are so many opportunities for you to share the enjoyment of re-living the Colonial era with those around you. Why not begin it all by contacting: Loudoun Museum and Information Center, 16 West Loudoun Street, Leesburg, VA 22075, 703/777-0519. They have turned out an excellent folder that gives the visitor a capsule of what there is of importance within the county to view. It is tied into a very helpful map that shows you what is where and how to get there. In point of fact, this is undoubtedly one of the best travel folders that we have ever seen. There are beautiful pictures and excellent graphics. Yet, we must

also give credit to our forefathers for putting so many wonderful sights into this county for our current day enjoyment.

BLUEMONT — A quiet rural community in the foothills of the Blue Ridge. It is the site of the annual Bluemont Fair. You won't want to miss it, if you are around on the third weekend of September.

UPPERVILLE — A quaint village in the heart of Virginia Hunt Country. The public is invited to visit many of the estates and breeding farms during the annual stable tour in mid-May. The Upperville Colt and Horseshow is held during the first week of June.

MIDDLEBURG — Called the unofficial capital of the "Hunt Country." This is undoubtedly one of the most picturesque communities to be found anywhere. This was a stagecoach stop between Alexandria and Winchester.

ALDIE — Well known grain mills from the late 1700's. This area was the scene of many of Mosby's raids during the Civil War. During the third weekend of October there is an annual Fall Harvest Festival.

OAK HILL — The residence of President James Monroe is partially visible from Route 15. Serves as a private residence and working farm. Open for group tours between April 15th until November 15th. Call Loudoun Information Center for information.

OATLANDS — A Greek Revival Mansion dates back to the 1805 era and was built for George Carter. Terraced formal gardens and mansions are on this working 260 acres estate. It is owned by the National Trust for Historic Preservation. Open to the public from early April until mid-November. Many community events are hosted here. Contact: Executive Director at 703/777-3174.

ROKEBY — This 18th Century home served as a secret depository for the United States Constitution and Declaration of Independence during the War of 1812. The home dates back to 1753 and is a private residence.

WASHINGTON DULLES AIRPORT — This modern facility is viewed by many each year. It is federally owned and operated.

BELMONT — A beautiful Georgian style mansion built around 1803. It is privately owned and is the site of the spring and fall steeplechase races of the Fairfax Hunt. Races are held the 3rd weekend of April and the 3rd Saturday after Labor Day.

MORVEN PARK — This Greek revival style mansion was built in the 1780's. This was the home of governors of two states; Thomas Swann of Maryland and Westmoreland Davis of Virginia. This is a 1200 acre estate with a magnificent mansion, extensive formal gardens, nature trails, and a carriage museum with more than 100 horse drawn vehicles on display. Numerous equestrian events are held here including the Fall National Hunt Steeplechase Races and the Carriage Drive Competition. Open weekends May through mid-October. Contact: Resident Manager 703/777-2414.

BALLS BLUFF — This is the smallest National Cemetery in the U.S. It marks the site of the fourth armed engagement of the Civil War. The cemetery is open for touring throughout the year. Booklet describing the battle may be obtained at the Loudoun Museum and Information Center.

WHITE'S FERRY — Beginning back in 1833 it was known as Conrad's Ferry. Passengers and freight were transported across the Potomac River by means of "poling" a small boat. In 1920, a hay bailer engine was used permitting two cars to cross at the same time. Today the "Gen. Jubal Early" transports up to six cars by a diesel powered tug. She makes the same daily crossings as did her name-sake 100 years ago. This provides quick and easy access to Loudoun County from the suburban Maryland countryside. Service is seven days a week from 6:00 AM until 11:00 PM excepting when the waters are high.

THE WORK HORSE MUSEUM — Located in Paeonian Springs; in this museum the work horse's contribution is commemorated. Displays of "tack" and farming implements span a period over 200 years. Included are farm implements, harnesses, blacksmith equipment, veterinarian supplies, plus a team of Clydesdale horses. Contact: Dr. Henry Buckhardt, President, The Work Horse Museum, Rt. 1, Box 77, Paeonian Springs, VA 22129, 703/338-6290.

WATERFORD — This small village was named after Waterford, Ireland and is the oldest in the county. It was founded in 1780. This was the home of Samuel Means who was Captain of the Loudoun Rangers, a band of Union sympathizers. Waterford and its greenbelt have been designated by the Department of the Interior as a National Historic Site. The Waterford Homes Tour and Craft Exhibit are held on the first weekend of October each year.

LINCOLN — A quaint rural village located south of Purcellsville with a rich Quaker tradition was settled in the early 1700's.

WESTERN ROUTE 7 CORRIDOR — At the turn of the 20th Century towns along this corridor were well known summer resorts. One can, today, note the Victorian architecture. Many of the area's residents continue the tradition of serving meals from locally grown fresh meats and produce picked in season.

SCENERY WITHOUT PEER — The rolling hills, the scenic countryside, and the picturesque rural communities make this one of the most pleasing regions of this or any other country. Early Scottish settlers named this "Little Scotland." Drink in the scenery. Capture it with either your brush or your camera.

LOVETTSVILLE — This town dates back to 1732, when it was a German settlement. During the Civil War many in this county remained loyal to the Union. Today there is a small museum and library housed in an old meat store of the 1900's.

MEREDYTH VINEYARDS — Open to the public. Located outside of Middleburg. Contact: P.O. Box 347, Middleburg, VA 22117, 703/687-6277.

PIEDMONT VINEYARDS — Open to the public. Located between the Plains and Middleburg on Va. 626. Contact: P.O. Box 286, Middleburg, VA 22117, 703/687-5134.

DRANESVILLE TAVERN — Five miles east of Loudoun on Route 7.

SULLY PLANTATION — Four miles south of Dulles on Route 28. Contact: 703/437-1794.

HARPERS FERRY — Contact: 304/535-6371

COLVIN RUN MILL PARK — Contact: 703/941-5000

ALGONQUIN REGIONAL PARK — Contact: 703/450-4655

RED ROCK WILDERNESS OVERLOOK REGIONAL PARK Contact: 703/278-8880.

MANASSAS BATTLEFIELD — Located some 10 miles from here is the Manassas National Battlefield Park. It was here that the first and second Battles of Manassas were fought. Information Center.

CALENDAR OF EVENTS — We suggest that you contact the Loudoun County Visitor's Center for a schedule of events. During the year there is always something of interest taking place in the county. Maybe it's a pottery making demonstration in Leesburg or a celebrity golf tournament or a national horseshow or even a basket weaving demonstration — maybe it's a race meet or maybe a sidewalk antique show. The point to remember is that it's a wonderful place to visit and there is always something going on. Once again the address is 16 W. Loudoun St., Leesburg, VA 22075, 703/777-0519.

While on the subject of things to see and do you might also be interested in visiting the Anituqe Center in Leesburg.

A WALK AROUND LEESBURG — Before departing Loudoun County we urge you to consider a walk through this historic town. Your walk will take you from the year 1750 to the present day. There is so much to see that any description that we might offer would fall far short of its desired objective. Why not secure a copy of the booklet as named above from the Loudoun Museum/Visitor Center. The booklet is so tastefully done and so very informative. We are certain that the booklet itself will be reason enough for you to make your pilgrimage to this charming village.

We realize that this effort to tell you about Loudoun County has omitted so much. But, space limits the ability to tell it all. Yet, we hope that we have imparted just enough information to start you on your visit to this interesting and historic section of the Old Dominion. When you have completed your sojourn here, we invite you to learn and enjoy more of this very fascinating and hospitable state.

— *Virginia State Travel Service*

Oatlands Plantation, Leesburg

LURAY

Lodgings: (703)
Cardinal Motel, E. Main St., 743-5010
Caverns Motel, Inc., 211 E. Main, 743-4575
Hillside Motel, US 211, 743-6322
Holiday Inn, US 211, By-pass, 743-5421
Intown Motel, 410 W. Main, 743-6511
Luray Caverns Motel East & West, Entrance Caverns, 743-6551
The Mimslyn Inn, 401 W. Main, 743-5105
Big Meadows Lodge, Skyline Dr., 999-2221
Skyline Lodge, Skyline Dr., 999-2221
Sherbrook Motel, 320 W. Main, 743-5176

Campgrounds
Mountain Manor Good Samparks, 743-4002
Skyline Drive Campground Info., 999-2266

Restaurants
Brookside Restaurant, US 211, 743-5698
Brown's Chinese & American Rest., 34 W. Main, 743-5630
Elaine's Restaurant & Ice Cream Parlor, 2 E. Main, 743-7400
Mamma's Kitchen, 42 E. Main, 743-4330
Sager's Family Restaurant, US 211, 743-6302
Shenandoah Room, US 211, 743-4521
The Parkhurst Inn Restaurant, US 211, 743-6009
Panorama Restaurant, US 211/Skyline Dr., 743-5108
Betty's Pizza Parlor, 606 E. Main, 743-3630
Caverns & Coach Restaurant, Luray Caverns, 743-6551
McDonald's, 709 E. Main, 743-6677
Arcade Lunch-Station Master, 43 W. Main, 743-3917
Big T Burger, US 211, 743-6196
Dan' Steak House, US 211, Massanutten Mtn., 743-6285
Intown Restaurant, 410 W. Main, 743-6511
Kentucky Fried Chicken, US 211, 743-4555
Sly Fox Restaurant, US 211, 743-6511

Sightseeing
LURAY CAVERNS — These caverns discovered in 1878 are among the best known in this country and receive countless visitors annually. In addition to the caverns, you are able to visit the Singing Tower with its carillon of 47 bells. The antique car and carriage caravan can also be viewed. A stalacpipe organ can be heard inside the caverns. For admission price information contact: 743-6551.

GUILDFORD RIDGE VINEYARD — Established in 1971; they grow a selection of French hybrid grapes. It is their hope to have their winery in production by the end of 1983.

RESTORED ONE ROOM SCHOOLHOUSE — This edifice is of interest and is open during the summer months between 12:00 Noon and 5:00 PM.

SHENANDOAH NATIONAL PARK — This very beautiful national treasure can be reached by taking US 22 east some few miles. This highway will intersect with the Skyline Drive. This Drive is 105 miles long and goes from Waynesboro to Front Royal. On the Drive are various waysides, lodgings, and other services. Visitors will be interested in learning of Skyland Lodge and Big Meadows Lodge as possible bases while visiting the Park. During off season reservations and information may be secured by calling 703/743-5108. During season call 703/999-2221. Information on Lewis Mountain Lodge can be secured by calling 703/999-2255 and the off season number 743-5108. Park and camping information should be addressed to Shenandoah National Park at Luray, VA 22835 or 703/999-2266.

RECREATION — Shenandoah River Outfitters, 743-4159, can supply you with canoes and other water activity needs.

CAVERNS COUNTRY CLUB — 743-6551, Golf, tennis, hiking, riding and swimming.

SHOPPING — The Pottery Barn & Factory, US 211.

FESTIVALS & SPECIAL EVENTS — Page Valley Fete Champetre. During the summer months there is an offering of outdoors concerts and theater. 778-3853.

PAGE VALLEY AGRICULTURAL & INDUSTRIAL FAIR — August. 743-3195.

SHENANDOAH NATIONAL PARK HOOVER DAYS — August. Hike tours and weekend retreat. 999-2243

PAGE COUNTY HERITAGE FESTIVAL — Crafts, house tours, pageant. 743-3195

CHRISTMAS IN LURAY — December. Parade, candlelit house tours. 743-3195

GENERAL INFORMATION — Luray is a town some 30 miles northeast of Harrisonburg. Population is about 4000. Altitude is 835 feet. The community enjoys four normal seasons and temperature is moderate and in keeping with the rest of the surrounding area.

NEW MARKET

Lodgings: (703)
Battlefield Motel, US 11, I-81, Ex. 67, 740-3105
Blue Ridge Motor Lodge, US 11, I-81, Ex. 67, 740-8088
Quality Inn-Shenandoah Valley, I-81, Ex. 67, 740-3141
Bryce Resort, Bayse, I-81, Ex. 69, 856-2121
Sky Chalet Country Inn, Bayse, I-81, Ex. 69, 856-2147
Best Western Inn-Mt. Jackson, I-81, Ex. 69, 477-2911
The Shenvalee, US 11, I-81, Ex. 67, 740-3181

Campgrounds:
Rancho Campground, 740-8313
Orkney Springs Campground, Orkney Springs, 856-2585

Dining:
Big Tee Burger, I-81, Ex. 67, 760-3614
Johnny Appleseed Restaurant & Lounge, I-81, Ex. 67, 740-3141
MD's Restaurant, US 11N, I-81, Ex. 67, 740-3730
The Shenvalee Restaurant & Lounge, US 11, I-81, Ex. 67, 740-3181
Southern Kitchen, US 11, I-81, Ex. 67, 740-3514

History

This small Valley community of approximately 1000 persons is steeped in history dating back to the early days of our country. When taking the walking tour of this community you are reviewing the beginnings which took place on the official recording date of New Market, December 14, 1796. The town's founder was General John Sevier, a famed Indian fighter of his time as well as Revolutionary patriot. It should be pointed out that John Sevier was to later become the first governor of the "Volunteer" State of Tennessee. It is in that state that a county and a city are named in his honor.

Etched in the history of the Civil War is the heroic action of the 247 teen-aged cadets from the Virginia Military Institute at the Battle of New Market. More than 10,000 soldiers engaged in combat here in 1864. This battle is re-enacted annually on the Sunday preceding the May 15th battle date.

Sightseeing

SHENANDOAH CAVERNS — The caverns are located approximately four miles north of New Market. It may be reached by getting off I-81 at Exit 68. Breathtaking best describes these caverns that veritably carry you from this world to a magic fairyland. Contact: 703/477-3115.

NEW MARKET BATTLEFIELD PARK & HALL OF VALOR Get off at I-81, Exit 67. This is a 160 acre battlefield park with its $2,000,000 museum commemorating the courage of the Virginia Military Institute cadets during the Civil War. Presented at the exhibit hall is an overview of the Civil War. Interesting color movies of 12 minutes and 16 minutes duration increase the value of the visit. Further information can be obtained by calling 703/740-3102.

TUTTLE & SPICE GENERAL STORE — Get off I-81 at Exit 68. Re-live the 1880's as you breathe the nostalgia in this yesteryear general store. This village store contains an authentic collection of Indian masks as well as artifacts from the era. This is a museum for the whole family. Gifts and candy are sold here.

SHENANDOAH VALLEY TOURIST INFORMATION CENTER — Visitors to the Shenandoah Valley will find a wealth of free information at their fingertips at this New Market location. Motorists can reach it by getting off at Exit 67 from I-81. The Center is owned and operated by the non-profit trade group, Shenandoah Valley Travel Association. Its membership is composed of firms engaged in tourism in the Shenandoah Valley extending from Harpers Ferry to Roanoke. This can be a very efficient way of finalizing your travel plans while visiting this area. For further information you may contact: Shenandoah Valley Travel Association, P.O. Box 488, New Market, VA 22844; 703/740-3132.

Potpourri

This town of 1000 persons is located in the southern tip of Shenandoah County. It is located approximately 18 miles north of Harrisonburg. Principal industries here are poultry and metal fabrication. New Market is registered as a historic district. A self guided 30 minute walking tour of the town will give you an opportunity to view a collection of interesting early 19th Century buildings.

SHENANDOAH VALLEY ACADEMY — A school for students from 9th to 12th grade is operated by the Seventh Day Adventist Church.

WINCHESTER

Lodgings: (703)
Best Western, Lee-Jackson Motor Inn, 711 Millwood Avenue, I-81,
 Ex. 80W on US 50W, 522N and 17N, 662-4154
Bond's Motel, 2930 Valley Avenue, US 11S, 667-8881
Echo Village Budget Motel, I-81, Ex. 79 on US 11S, 869-1900
Elms Motel, 2011 Valley Avenue, I-81, Ex. 79 on US 11S, 662-2567
The Farm Motel, US 50E/340N, Boyce, Va., 837-1692
Holiday Inn East, I-81, Ex. 80E on US 50E, 667-3300
Holiday Inn South, I-81, Ex. 79 on US 11S, 667-1200
Howard Johnson's Motor Lodge, I-81, Ex. 82/US 11N, 667-3802
Mountain View Motel, US 50E, Millwood, Va., 837-1222
Quality Inn Boxwood South, 2649 Valley Ave., I-81, Ex. 79 on
 US 11S, 662-2521
Quality Inn East/Duff's, 603 Millwood Avenue, I-81, Ex. 80W on
 US 50W, 522N and 17N, 667-2250

Campgrounds: (703)
Battle of Cedar Creek, Middletown, Va., 869-9856
Candy Hill, US 50W, 662-8010
The Cove, Gore, Va., 858-2882

Dining: (703)
Abe's Essenhaus, adjacent to Elms Motel, 2011 Valley Avenue, I-81,
 Ex. 79 on US 11S, 662-8386
Aiken's Sizzling Steaks, 2828 Valley Ave., I-81, Ex. 79 on US 11S,
 667-2828
Duff's Rebel Restaurant and The Cabaret Nightclub, adjacent to
 Quality Inn East/Duff's, 601 Millwood Ave., I-81, Ex. 80W on
 US 50W, 522N and 17N, 662-2571
Duff's Restaurant, adjacent to Quality Inn Boxwood South, 2655
 Valley Ave., I-81, Ex. 79 on US 11S, 667-8311
The Farm Restaurant, adjacent to The Farm Motel, US 50E/340N,
 Boyce, Va., 837-1692
Golden Corral Family Steak House, 2601 Valley Ave., I-81, Ex. 79
 on US 11S, 667-6329
Howard Johnson's Restaurant, adjacent to Howard Johnson's
 Motor Lodge, I-81, Ex. 82/US 11N, 667-3802
Kentucky Fried Chicken of Stephens City, I-81, Ex. 78, 869-4110
Kentucky Fried Chicken of Winchester, 1042 Berryville Ave., I-81,
 Ex. 81, 667-0212
Lee-Jackson Restaurant, adjacent to Best Western, Lee-Jackson
 Motor Inn, 711 Millwood Ave., I-81, Ex. 80W on US 50W, 522N
 and 17N, 662-4154
McDonald's Restaurant, 6 Valley Ave., US 50W/11S, 667-0033
McDonald's Restaurant, I-81, Ex. 82/US 11N, 667-6036

Manuel's and Wife Restaurant, adjacent to Holiday Inn South, I-81, Ex. 79 on US 11S, 662-1192

Mason's Seafood, 242 Millwood Ave., I-81, Ex. 80W on US 50W, 522N and 17N, 662-6093

Michel's, Sunnyside Station, US 522N, 667-9797

Open Hearth Restaurant, located in Holiday Inn East, I-81, Ex. 80E on 50E, 667-3300

WINCHESTER: A DAY OF DISCOVERY

by Elaine Hall, Mabel Landers, Donna Boyce

As I approached Winchester, located at the top of Virginia and gateway to the beautiful and historic Shenandoah Valley, I was reminded that, as many Americans who, in moving south and west, came through this valley in the mid-1700's, I, too, was drawn to this colorful corridor, so conveniently located near the picturesque Skyline Drive. Some of my own ancestors, perhaps, settled for a few years before seeking new frontiers, while others may have braved the hostile environment of the French and Indian War to settle permanently. As my interstate fatigue took its toll, I turned the car off I-81 at exit 80 west for some fresh air and a new perspective.

Joist Hite, a German from Pennsylvania, along with sixteen families, came in 1732 as Winchester's first settlers. They made their home a few miles south of the Shawnee Indian camping grounds. Quakers, led by Alexander Ross, came about the same time and built Hopewell Meeting House near Clearbrook, Virginia. I was a similar type of traveler, a tourist looking for a peaceful place to be.

As I left I-81 onto US 50 West, I came to Abram's Delight, or the Hollingsworth House. It is a lovely testimony of the past built of natural limestone, in 1754, by Isaac Hollingsworth, son of Abraham, a Quaker from Maryland. Beautifully restored, the house is furnished in appropriate style, with boxwood gardens completing the delightful setting.

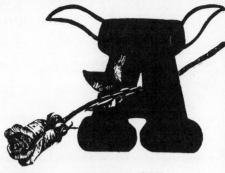

Aikens **is**

GREAT STEAKS!

Family-Owned Chain — Just 9 Years Old!

VIRGINIA	WEST VIRGINIA
2828 Valley Avenue Winchester, Va.	306 Wilson Street Martinsburg, WV
301 Fort Evans Road Leesburg, Va.	1430 Edwin Miller Blvd. Martinsburg, WV

Aikens Sizzling Sirloin Strip

Plus T-Bone, Ribeyes, Sirloins and our one of a kind Combination Meals: Steak and Ribs, Steak and Shrimp/Clams.

SEAFOOD AND CHICKEN ENTREES • OPEN SALAD BAR

Plus . . .

OUR NEWEST STORE!

Pancakes • Omelettes • Waffles
BIG STEAKS • GREAT SEAFOOD
Full Bar Service

 **. . . fine dining at reasonable prices!**
Interstate 81 Exit   (Rt. 50)

I continued on scenic Pleasant Valley Road, along the western edge of Winchester's Municipal Park, where Fall was at its most lovely in colors of varied hue. I turned onto National Avenue, where I saw what is probably the first national cemetery — dedicated in 1866.

Turning towards town, on East Piccadilly Street, stands the Old Stone Presbyterian Church. General Daniel Morgan, of Morgan's Riflemen fame, was a member. He was buried in the Church's graveyard in 1802 but his remains were transferred to nearby Mount Hebron Cemetery at the end of the War Between the States. I recalled that the guide at Abram's had told me that Morgan's home on Amherst Street was privately owned, so I could only hope to view it in passing. To learn more about Morgan, local history and the possibility of tracing my genealogy, I stopped briefly to peruse the records available for research in the Archives of the Handley Library at the corner of Piccadilly and Braddock Streets. The unique Beaux-arts building, built in 1913, was a bequest of Judge John Handley of Scranton, Pennsylvania, a patron of Winchester.

A member of the library staff urged me to continue on Piccadilly street to Fairmont Avenue and on to Confederate General Thomas Jonathan "Stonewall" Jackson's 1861-1862 winter headquarters, located on Braddock Street. I found the headquarters, built in 1854, to be a fine example of Hudson River Gothic Revival architecture. How fortunate for the general that Mrs. Jackson was able to join him in Winchester for three months to lighten the grim overtones of the War Between the States.

The general's office looked much as it must have then: his desk, his field chest, a prayer table and other memorabilia; even the wallpaper has been faithfully reproduced for authenticity. I saw artifacts belonging to such figures as Jed Hotchkiss, Jackson's mapmaker of the valley, General Turner Ashby of the cavalry, and Dr. Hunter Holmes McQuire, Jackson's medical director, which jogged memories of history lessons.

I walked the eight blocks to the Stonewall Confederate Cemetery, a part of Mount Hebron Cemetery. From the majestic gate house, adjacent to the old Lutheran Church ruins, a groundskeeper emerged. His enlightening conversation taught me that the ladies of Winchester were responsible for reburying the three thousand Confederate dead brought to Winchester in 1866 from as far away as fifteen miles. Among those resting there were General Turner Ashby and his brother, Captain Richard Ashby, as well as ancestors of the famed General George Patton of World War II.

I drove the four blocks south from Jackson's Headquarters on Braddock Street to its intersection with Cork Street to George Washington's Office. Washington used this structure while directing the building of Fort Loudoun during the French and Indian War. I learned that he came to Winchester in 1748, as a sixteen year old surveyor for Lord Fairfax. Washington remained in Winchester until 1758, receiving his militia training by protecting Virginia's three hundred mile frontier, while using Winchester from which to stage his four expeditions against the French in the French and Indian War. Twice, he was elected from Winchester to serve in the legislature of Colonial Virginia, the House of Burgesses.

Underscoring the image of Winchester as a city rich in heritage, I discovered a tree-lined, pedestrian mall, designated "Old Town Winchester," where the historical and traditional flavor has been preserved for modern shoppers. A local merchant drew my attention to the 1840 Frederick County Courthouse, still in use, and to the oldest active pharmacy in the United States, both facing onto the mall.

As I left the city to continue on my scheduled route, passing modern businesses, restaurants, lodging facilities and urban shopping centers, I marvelled at how pleasantly I had spent my day in a city where past and present mingle graciously; and as the twilight shadows gathered, I vowed to return to Winchester to experience more of its heritage and to explore the beautiful surrounding countryside.

The SPRING HOUSE

Just 30 Minutes Down the Valley To Woodstock

SALAD BAR — 41 ITEMS

HOMEMADE SOUP

Mobil Travel Guide Rated

Come join us in a Relaxed and Charming Atmosphere for something from our extensive menu. Virtually everything is made by us, from the rolls and desserts to the salad dressings and special salads on our salad bar.

Our Log Lounge is open daily.

1983
SILVER SPOON AWARD
GDCB

Open 7 days a week
Serving Breakfast, Lunch and Dinner

325 S. Main St.   Woodstock, Va.   703-459-4755

Geography
Winchester is located in the northwestern part of the state some 72 miles from Washington, D.C.; 98 miles from Baltimore; 90 miles from Charlottesville and 140 miles from Richmond. The city serves as county seat for Frederick County. The inter-relationship between the two political entities is extremely close in all activities.

The rolling hills and verdant meadowlands make this a landscape painter's paradise. Elevation here is about 720 feet.

Though there is a diversification of industry, traditionally, it is agriculturally oriented. Apples and apple products have always played a key part in the economy. In addition to the foregoing, plastic and furniture manufacturing is finding its place. Included in the menu of products manufactured are auto parts, brake linings, cans, concrete forms and blocks, clay, garments, conveyor belts, glass sand, shoe heels and soles. The list includes such items as limestone, manganese, type matrices, frozen foods, trailers, records and drugs that contribute to the prosperity of the community.

Climate
The area enjoys four seasons of moderate climate. During the summer months there will be some days of 90 degree temperature and conversely during the winter there will be several periods of snow.

Logistics
The community is blessed with numerous highways: I-81, US 522, US 50, and State 7 take care of the motorist. The nearest commercial airport is Dulles International located some 50 miles distant. Washington National is some 20 miles further. Greyhound takes care of the bus requirements.

Population
Total combined population for Frederick County and the City of Winchester is 54,000. Of that number 20,000 live in the city. Reflecting the growth and prosperity of the area is the reassuring fact that the county registered a gain of 40% in the census of 1980 over 1970.

Education
Shenandoah College and Conservatory of Music is a liberal arts institution with a very well established music curriculum.

Festivals
SHENANDOAH APPLE BLOSSOM FESTIVAL — At this writing it has been held 56 times. It is held traditionally on the weekend nearest to the 1st of May. Keep in mind that this can fall in April as well as May. This gala extravaganza lasting four days is highlighted by the Grand Feature Parade. It is reputed to be the third longest in the United States — number one being the Macy's and the second

being the Rose Bowl. This nationally televised attraction will feature a grand marshal of prominence. Marching in the parade will be more than 80 bands coming from as many as 27 states. There will be more than 50 floats on display in this 4½ hour parade.

In addition to the above mentioned parade, there are various contests and pageants taking place. Winchester becomes alive with celebrities and dignitaries for the many festivities and events. There are band contests, arts and crafts shows, musical entertainment and plenty of excitement in general. For further information you can contact: Festival Headquarters, P.O. Box 3099, Winchester, VA 22601.

MOUNTAIN HERITAGE ARTS & CRAFTS FESTIVAL — This is held near Harpers Ferry, West Virginia. They generally have one festival in September and another in June. They have about 175 skilled craftsmen demonstrating and selling their wares. Folk dancing, folk singing, apple butter making are part of the festival. Contact: 304/725-2055.

APPLE HARVEST ARTS & CRAFTS FESTIVAL is held each September.

EDINBURG OLD TIME FESTIVAL is held in September.

In addition to the above, the following annual events are on tap: March—Kernstown Memorial Weekend; April—Apple Blossom Antique Car Show; Historic Garden Week; May—Semi-annual Civil War Show; National Skirmish-North-South Skirmish Association; June—Art Experience; July—Shenandoah Valley Farm Craft Days; Steam & Gas Engine Show; August—Frederick County Youth Fair; October—Semi-annual Civil War Show; National Skirmish; December—Historic Christmas Tours-Abram's Delight, Stonewall Jackson's Headquarters, Belle Grove Plantation. Christmas Tours of private homes.

Specific details can be secured from the Winchester-Frederick County Chamber of Commerce, 2 N. Cameron Steet, Winchester, VA 22601, 703/662-4118. We find the people at this office to be enthusiastic, knowledgeable, and extremely cordial.

There are numerous events in the area that you should investigate when you plan your visit to the area. As example, we mention the following: Woodstock—July: Shenandoah Valley Music Festival, 459-3396; August—Shenandoah County Fair, 459-3867.

Further information on special events on a regional basis can always be secured from the Virginia Division of Tourism, 202 N. Ninth St., Suite 500, Richmond, VA 23219, 804/786-2051.

BASEBALL — During the months of June and July baseball fans can be treated to a very interesting brand of ball. The Shenandoah Valley League entrant, Winchester Royals, is made up of college students aspiring towards major league contracts. The facility where they play their games, Bridgeforth Field, is unusual for a town this size.

Sightseeing
The visitor to Winchester quickly realizes that the history of this nation continues to be portrayed from its earlier times. The unusual architecture calls one back to earlier times. Let us review some of the many points of interest of these early years:

STONEWALL JACKSON'S HEADQUARTERS located on North Braddock Street is currently a museum open from April through October.

SHERIDAN'S HEADQUARTERS at the corner of Picadilly & Braddock. Private.

DANIEL MORGAN'S HOME (Hero of the Revolution) Amherst Street. Private.

LORD FAIRFAX'S TOMB — Christ Episcopal Church yard; Boscawen and Washington.

WASHINGTON'S OFFICE — Museum open April through October. Cork and Braddock.

HANDLEY SCHOOL — Public school partially endowed by Judge John Handley is the only privately endowed public school in the state. The facade is styled in a Jeffersonian motif. The school is located on a beautiful campus and is a local showplace. It is located on Valley Avenue.

ABRAM'S DELIGHT — Dates back to 1754 and is fully restored. April-October. Pleasant Valley Road.

STONEWALL CEMETERY — The Confederate War dead are buried in a section of the Mount Hebron Cemetery.

NATIONAL CEMETERY — Union dead are buried here.

OLD STONE PRESBYTERIAN CHURCH — Built in 1788, the interior is an example of churches of the Colonial era. Open daily with no admission charge.

Note: The above cemeteries, churches, and several other points of interest are concentrated in Woodstock.

FREDERICK COUNTY COURTHOUSE erected in 1840 N. Louden St. Mall.

WINCHESTER-FREDERICK COUNTY HISTORICAL SOCIETY: 662-6550

Archival Section of the Handley Library.

We refer serious minded individuals to the above reliable sources of historical information for this region. It is also suggested that those individuals desirous of having privately escorted tours contact the Chamber of Commerce in advance of arrival.

Out-Of-Town Points of Interest

You are in the beautiful Shenandoah Valley of Virginia which for hundreds of years before was inhabited by the Indians. They named the valley SHENANDOAH, which translates to "daughter of the stars."

SPRINGDALE — This fine stone house built in 1753 is on US 11 at Bartonsville some six miles south of Winchester, on the east side of the road.

MIDDLETOWN — A very quaint town in the heart of "horse country" that should not be omitted form your itinerary. Sheridan's troops were here during the Civil War. The general, himself, occupied the Belle Grove mansion which is located a mile south of Middletown. The house which was built in 1794 stands in the middle of the Cedar Creek Battlefield. Belle Grove is open to the public. Further information: 869-2028.

The town is home of the Wayside Foundation for the Arts. They are involved in professional Summer Theater, theater workshops, and in the restoring of St. Thomas Church, which was built in 1835.

BATTLES AT KERNSTOWN — US 11, two miles south of Winchester.

THE BURWELL-MORGAN MILL is located at Millwood and is located on Va. 255 one mile north of US 50. This is 12 miles east of Winchester. The mill construction began in 1782 and remained in operation until 1953. In 1963 restoration of this wonderful example of 18th Century technology was begun. For further information concerning the mill call: 837-1556.

SHENANDOAH NATIONAL PARK — The Skyline Drive extends from Front Royal and may be reached from Winchester by US 522.

STRASBURG — If you are a Civil War buff, you will find this to be a very interesting place. The signal corps sent "wigwag" messages from nearby Signal Knob and flashed heliograph messages from one mountain peak to the next. The Battle of Fisher's Hill was fought two miles south of town. To the north of town stands the Hupp Homestead which was built in 1755.

Historic 1848
EDINBURG MILL
Restaurant
featuring
· DAILY HEARTY COUNTRY BUFFETS ·
· PLUS FULL MENU ·
· GIFT SHOP · ART GALLERY ·
· COCKTAIL LOUNGE ·

OPEN DAILY 7 a.m.-10 pm.

Edinburg, VA
EXIT 71 off
I-81

phone:
(703) 984-8555

STRASBURG MUSEUM is located in the former Southern Railway depot. Inside the museum are artifacts of local life here during the 18th and 19th Centuries as well as Indian artifacts and fossils. On an adjoining side track you can also view an old caboose.

WOODSTOCK — County seat of Shenandoah County. It was here that the Reverend Peter Muhlenbuerg parted with his ministerial vestments and took up the sword. He recruited a German regiment and also joined the Continental Army and was considered to be a genius in military tactics. He commanded a brigade at Brandywine and Yorktown as well as other Revolutionary battles.

OBSERVATION TOWER — On top of Massanutten Mountain. To get there you turn left at the old courthouse and follow the winding road along the mountainside. A spectacular scenic view rewards your efforts.

MASSANUTTEN MILITARY ACADEMY is located here.

NEW MARKET — This town is discussed in greater detail under Harrisonburg. New Market Battlefield and the Hall of Valor should be visited.

Two and one half miles south are the ENDLESS CAVERNS. Four miles south of town is COURT MANOR PLANTATION. It is a

working Angus cattle and horse ranch. MELROSE CAVERNS are 10 miles south of town. It is at these caverns that the famed Kilroy of World War II fame got the idea for the inscription of his name all over Europe. Within the caverns are thousands of names of soldiers from both sides during the Civil War. Neither Endless nor Melrose Caverns are open to the public.

— *Virginia State Travel Service*
Skyline Drive, in the Blue Ridge Mountains of Virginia

DEAR JOHN AND JOAN: COME VISIT THE MOUNTAINS

By Mary Toy

My husband, Jim and I moved to Fishersville, Virginia in late 1982 from St. Louis, Missouri. Neither of us had visited western Virginia before this move. Following is a description of our experience in "Virginia — the Western Highlands" as written to friends in St. Louis.

July 15, 1983

Dear John and Joan:

Well, here we are in western Virginia. If there's one word to describe this area, it's mountains. Everything and everybody here is colored by them. Few people seem to want to leave and the ones who do appear to yearn to get back to "their" mountains.

Don't misunderstand, the Alleghenies and the Blue Ridge haven't produced a region of sameness. The people defined by them are as diverse as the differences between a Jeffersonian scholar and a coal miner. It's just that the diversity has a common thread — the mountains.

I'm afraid Jim and I are having midwestern withdrawal symptoms, though. Not a major league baseball game to be found. College basketball is the key sport. Texas Longhorn fans have absolutely no team spirit when compared to the devotion of Virginia fans to University of Virginia Cavalier Basketball. Maybe that, too, is caused by the mountains. People are used to looking up at things and they do look up at UVA's basketball players. I think last year's basketball superstar, Ralph Sampson, was 7'4". Anyway, if you're not a basketball fan, you'd better become one or be resigned to just smiling and nodding during a lot of conversations.

Have you ever been to a tractor pull? Neither had we until last week. Tractor pulls also inspire devotion in the western part of Virginia. I'll admit, we had a real good time at the one we went to. Sleds weighing up to 50,000 pounds are attached to the back of tractors. The winning tractor (or pick-up truck) is the one that can pull the sled the farthest on a muddy track. It's a thrill when those tractors get running, the black smoke starts pouring out of them and the noise starts to build. I found myself rooting for *all* the tractors —along with just about everybody else in the crowd. In between pulls, there's also the fun of hickory smoked barbeque and bluegrass music.

Jim and I got our first real taste of bluegrass on the opening day of trout season. I never realized that trout fishing was such a big thing. Just watching people's anticipation of, and preparation for, the important day was a delight. Everywhere we went, from the grocery store to the doctor's office, we found somebody talking about trout fishing. It doesn't even matter if you fish, just heading up to a trout stream is like going to a carnival. All ages are represented from toddlers to great-great-great grandparents and you're likely to hear some good pickin', sip some good whiskey and generally have a fine old time.

Both of us have been converted to bluegrass music and pickin' and singin' after our trout experience. It's not uncommon to find whole families who enjoy nothing better than to sit around harmonizing in impromptu gatherings. Usually, everyone plays at least two instruments, the guitar and the mandolin. Most times, at least one or two people also play the fiddle, the banjo and the steel guitar. It's amazing to watch one person start playing a tune on a guitar for a few minutes and then to see five other people, one by one, pick up on the tune and start embellishing it. By the time the song is over, you know you've just heard a never-to-be-forgotten musical event. Nobody is just performing, the musicians are getting as much of a "kick" as their audience, if there even is an audience. I always berated myself for not having a tape recorder with me at all times.

I hope you haven't gotten the idea that western Virginia is full of tractor-pulling basketball fans who fish and play music. I've never seen so many good schools all in one area. Within the vicinity are Washington and Lee, James Madison, Virginia Tech, Bridgewater College, Eastern Mennonite College and Mary Baldwin College. Mary Baldwin is in Staunton (that's pronounced stanton) and is a former women's college that is now co-ed. Mary Baldwin's campus is what I imagined college would be like when I was a little girl. There's the peaceful, hushed white halls, high ceilings and old wood, the curving staircases, the old pictures of academic ancestors, the cool marble, and the geometric black and white tiled entranceways. Judy Garland and Mickey Rooney would have gone to school here in one of their "Babes" movies.

Of course, the most well-known school is the University of Virginia (UVA) in Charlottesville. UVA was founded by Thomas Jefferson and the school still strives to live up to Jefferson's precepts and theories about an academic village.

Charlottesville is one of the few places which turns out to look exactly the way you'd imagine it would look. Yes, the University has picture-postcard buildings that Thomas Jefferson designed and lived in. Yes, the horse country surrounding the city is full of beautiful ante-bellum homes. And, yes, Charlottesville is the home of "prep," the land of blue blazers and khaki skirts. The "prep," though, seems fitting. Everyone looks comfortable, neat and happy to be living in Charlottesville. With the mountains as a backdrop for all this history, education and elegance, it's no wonder Jefferson and Madison made their homes here. Neither Thomas Jefferson nor Walt Disney could have designed a more fitting stage setting for the City of Charlottesville.

"Over the mountain" (as Jim and I learned to say) from Charlottesville is the Shenandoah Valley which lies between the Blue Ridge and the Allegheny mountains. The valley is breathtaking —especially in the springtime. "A drive along the Blue Ridge Parkway or Skyline Drive is a must in the springtime," we were told time and again. It's true. We never got tired of seeing the mountain ivy, wild rhododendron, mountain laurel and dogwood (illegal to pick in Virginia). Besides, it's cool up there. On the spring day we took our first drive the temperature in the Valley was 85°F. The Parkway still had snow on the shoulder of the road. Of course, even in other seasons, the view from 2800 feet up is not something to be overlooked.

An interesting trip we took about three weeks ago was to southwestern Virginia. The mountains of southwestern Virginia dominate the lives of the people they surround as nowhere else we visited in the western part of the state. Mining the coal from these mountains provide many people here with their only source of income. The mountains seem closer. They seem a part of every activity however routine. These mountains are also rounder, older, less austere, less grandiose and wilder than those further north.

The phase "God's Country" comes immediately to mind in southwestern Virginia. The mountains shelter people who believe in a fundamental God, in fire and brimstone, in the evils of liquor, tobacco and dancing. But, they also believe in a God who says "take care of one another." Even in the pockets of poverty caused when the coal ran out, you will find families making sure neighbors and strangers who need food are fed.

The roads that cut through southwestern Virginia were a shock after the straight and well-maintained highway system of central and northern Virginia. These wildly winding roads follow the path of the mountains. Driving them for the first time is an adventure — especially when you hit curves that would be U-turns in the city.

Many of the towns in this part of the state are "dry" meaning the sale of liquor is illegal. Rumor has it that the mountains continue to hide stills and bootleggers. Most often, however, modern day bootleggers are involved in running not corn whiskey, but rum, vodka, gin, tequila and blended bourbons. We couldn't find a neighborhood liquor distributor, though. People here are friendly, but not *that* friendly (or naive).

There's so much more I could tell you. Virginia has a deep sense of history and you'll find historical markers everywhere. Monticello,

New Market Battlefield, Woodrow Wilson's birthplace, the Barter Theatre and the home of James Madison are just a few of the local historical attractions.

Virginians also have a deep sense of the dollar. Factory outlet stores (such as Cannon Towel and Wrangler factory outlets) can be found in almost every town. Then there are the little interesting sidelights such as the fact that Culpeper, VA, hides deep underground the federal reserve system's vault and offices that are built to survive a nuclear attack. (They say that provisions at the vault even include a system to reimburse money-market fund holders should any be around after a nuclear war).

There's so much more to tell you that I have to stop somewhere so I'll stop here. I only hope that this letter will whet your appetite to come visit and get to know the part of Virginia to which we've become so attached.

Love,
Jim and Mary

— Virginia State Travel Service

Thomas Jefferson's "Academical Village," Heart of the University of Virginia at Charlottesville

REGION 2

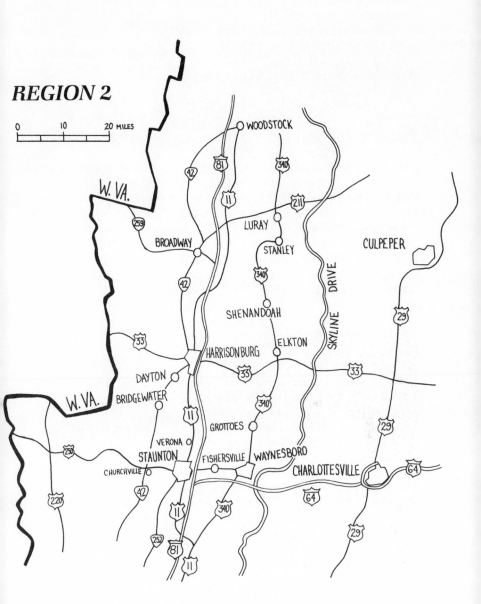

CHARLOTTESVILLE
Dining: (804)
American
Aberdeen Barn, 2018 Holiday Dr., 296-4630
Adams, Ramada US 29N, 977-7700
The Big Ladle, 404 Water, 295-4420
Blue Moon Diner, 512 W. Main, 293-3408
Boar's Head Inn, US 250W, 296-2181
The Brown Derby, 1522 E. High, 296-2203
C. K. Restaurant, 1327 W. Main, 295-7706
Charley's, N. Wing, Barracks Rd. Spg. Ctr., 293-5124
Christian's, McIntire Plaza, 293-3000
Claire's, 11 Elliewood Ave., 295-3418
The Cotton Exchange, 817 W. Main, 295-7050
Court Square Tavern, 500 Court Square, 296-6111
Curly's Garage, US 29N, Shopper's World, 973-1839
Duner's, US 250W, Ivy, 293-8352
Dutch Pantry Restaurant, 1615 Emmett St., 296-1922
Dutch Treat, N. Wing Barracks Rd. Spg. Ctr., 295-6537
Friendly Family Restaurant, Fashion Sq. Mall, 973-6837
Gaslight Restaurant, 625 W. Main, 296-1249
Gola's Mountain View Restaurant, US 250W, 823-4460
Graffiti, 16 Elliewood Ave., 296-2260
Hardware Store Restaurant, 316 E. Main, 977-1518
Hilltop Inn Restaurant, US 250E, 296-6069
Hollymead Inn, US 29N, 973-8488
Howard Johnson's Restaurant, 1309 W. Main, 296-1994
The Ivy Inn, 2244 Old Ivy Rd., 977-1222
Jake's Place, N. Wing Barracks Rd. Shp. Ctr., 971-4696
Kettle Restaurant & Pancake House, 129 N. Emmett, 977-9433
Lord Hardwicke Inn, 1248 Emmett, 295-6668
Michie Tavern—An 18th Century Ordinary, Rte. 53, 977-1234
Miller's, On-the-Mall, 971-8511
Mousetrap, 14th & W. Main, 296-6873
Muldowney's Restaurant, 212 W. Water St., 296-8783
The New Jockey Club, Quality Inn, US 250E, 977-2811
The Nook, 415 E. Main, 293-2595
Pan & Pantry, Albemarle Square, US 29N, 973-1724
Pancake Pantry, 1817 Emmett St., 295-9490
Picadilly Pub, English Inn, 971-9900
Piper's, Holiday Inn North, US 29N, 293-9111
Piper's, Holiday Inn South, I-64, 5th St. Ex., 977-5100
Random Row Restaurant, 247 Ridge McIntire, 296-8758
Red River Rib Co., 1240 Seminole Trail, 973-7427
The Roasted Bean & The Abbie, 110 4th St. NE, 977-5282
Shoney's, Albemarle Sq., US 29N, 973-4309

Shoney's, 1900 Arlington Blvd., 295-4196
The Tavern, 1140 Emmett St., 295-0404
Thatcher's, 2244 Ivy Rd., 295-1315
Tony's Chuckwagon Restaurant, E. High & US 250 By-pass,
    977-9714
    119 4th St., N.E., 296-6509
The Virginian Restaurant, 1521 W. Main, 293-2606
Western Sizzlin' Steak House, 1250 Seminole Trail, 973-3324

Cafeteria Service
Bonanza Family Restaurant, 1525 E. Rio Rd., 973-5798
Ken Johnson's Cafeteria, Barracks Rd. Shopping Ctr., 293-9324
Morrison's Cafeteria, Fashion Sq. Mall, 973-4359
University Cafeteria, 1517 W. Main, 293-3242

Continental
C & O Restaurant, 515 E. Water St., 971-7044
The Galerie, US 250W, 823-5883
The Garret, 14th & W. Main, 295-6060
Le Snail Patisserie, 633 W. Main, 295-9203
Le Snail Restaurant, 320 W. Main, 295-4456
Schnitzelhouse Restaurant, 2208 Fontaine Ave., 293-7185

Delicatessen
Littlejohn's New York Delicatessen, 1427 W. Main, 977-0588
Macado's, 1505 W. Main, 971-3558
Wayside Deli, 2200 Jefferson Pk. Ave., 295-1278

Italian
Anna's Restaurant, 115 Maury Ave., 977-6228
Dennis Restaurant, N. Wing Barracks Rd., 293-5974
Expresso International Restaurant, 1202 W. Main, 295-0338
Fellini's, 200 W. Market, 295-8003
Sal's Pizza & Italian Restaurant, Shopper's World, 973-3339
Sbarro, The Italian Eatery, Fashion Sq. Mall, 973-1948
Tony's Pizza & Italian Restaurant, Albemarle Sq., 973-4601

Mexican
Fiesta Cantina, 1258 Emmett St., 293-8411
La Hacienda, 400 Emmett St., 295-0258
Lena's Dance Restaurant,, 20 Elliewood, 293-6900
Margarita's, 1429 University Ave., 971-8346

International
Eastern Standard, Downtown Mall, 295-8668
Zandi's French Bakery, Woodbrook Village, 973-2947

Oriental/Polynesian/Japanese/Chinese
Aloha Resaurant, US 250E, 977-1779
Chinese Dragon, US 29S, 295-1935
The Japanese Steak House, 4 Seasons Dr., 973-8080
The Mandarin, 1250 Emmet St., 295-3044
The Ming Dynasty, 1417 Emmet St., 979-0909
Peking Tea House, US 250W, 296-3023
Piney Mountain Resaurant, US 29N, 973-3186
Szechuan Resaurant, 2006 Holiday Dr., 296-9090
Taiwan Garden, 9 University Shopping Ctr., 295-0081

Pizza & Subs
Archie's Pizza, 2508 Fontaine, 293-2265
Barnaby's, 395 Greenbrier Dr., US 29N, 973-8346

1417 Emmet Street
Charlottesville, VA 22901

SAM JEAN
(804) 979-0909

The **Ming Dynasty**

RESTAURANT AND LOUNGE

CHINESE CUISINE

Domino's Pizza, 722 Rio Rd., 973-1243
   1137 Millmont St., 971-8383
Lupo's, 280 Emmet St., 296-7007
Noel's Sub Shop, 13 Univ. Shopping Ctr., 977-2611
Noel's Too, Shopper World, 973-7983
Pizza Hut, 1300 Emmet St., 977-7190
   1718 Seminole Trail, 973-1616
Pizza Inn, US 29N, 973-3321
Pizza Jake, Albemarle Sq., 973-5108
TJ's Pub, 14th St. Mall, 977-8814
Tubby's, 1412 E. High, 293-3825

Seafood
Family Fish House, Shopper's World, 973-5391
Monticello Room, 500 Court Sq., 296-6111
That Seafood Place, 105 Emmet St., 293-2211
Tiffany's Seafood Restaurant, Univ. Shopping Ctr., 293-5000

Fast Food
Arby's, 1230 Emmet, 296-8995
Bixby's, 502 E. Market, 296-2712
The Burger House, Avon St., 293-7116
Burger King, 1609 University, 977-4785
The Caravan, US 29N, 973-6569
Charlie's Fried Chicken & Taters, 2nd & Water, 296-3217
Chik Fil A, Fashion Sq. Mall, 973-1646
Chili Shop, 1395 W. Main, 296-1937
El Cabrito's, Hydraulic Rd., 973-4289
   1415 University Ave., 971-9915
Golden Skillet Fried Chicken, 1551 E. High, 977-0392
Hardee's, 2025 Ivy Rd., 977-5550
   US 250E, 977-3191
   US 29N, 973-2083
Jak n Jill, 1404 E. High, 293-7213
Kentucky Fried Chicken, US 29N, 295-5158
   600 Cherry Ave., 296-1475

THE BOAR'S HEAD INN
ONE OF AMERICA'S
TRULY GREAT INNS

A country estate atmosphere has been created for you in the foothills of the Blue Ridge Mountains of Virginia.

175 guest rooms filled with country charm, a grand ballroom, 3 dining rooms, beautifully landscaped grounds, and a private Sports Club with extensive year round health and recreational facilities. And golf will be available to guests with the opening of The Birdwood Golf Course in the spring of 1984. The course is an 18-hole, par 72 championship course and is immediately adjacent to the Sports Club.

Plan to stay at "One of America's Truly Great Inns"... you will delight in the many special events, challenge yourself to a variety of resort sports and relax in the unequalled beauty of the Inn's surroundings.

For reservations, brochure or calendar of events:

 **THE BOAR'S HEAD INN**

John Rogan, President

Dept. LM
P.O. Box 5185
Charlottesville, VA 22905
Phone: 804-296-2181

The Korner Restaurant, 413 9th, 977-9535
Long John Silver, 1254 Emmet St., 977-3665
Luv n Oven, Scottsville, 286-3830
McDonald's, Ridge-McIntire, 977-2984
   Barracks Road Shopping Center, 295-6092
   Fashion Square Mall, 973-5921
Pig Tails Bar BQ, 1403 Emmet, 971-7635
The Orange Bowl, Fashion Sq. Mall, 973-8217
Rising Sun Bakery, 109 14th St., NW, 296-2233
Roy Rogers Family Resaurant, US 29N, 295-8874
Silver Grill, Scottsville, 286-2364
Swiss Pretzel Shop, Fashion Sq. Mall, 973-1588
Wayside Take Out, 2203 Jefferson Pk., 977-5000
Wendy's, US 29N, 973-6226
   Preston & McIntire

CHARLOTTESVILLE: (804)

Lodging:
Airport Motel, US 29N, 973-5978
Best Western Cavalier, US 250/US 29, 296-8111
Best Western Mount Vernon, US 29N, 296-5501
The Boar's Head Inn, US 250W, 296-2181
The Cardinal Motel, US 29N, 293-6188
Crossroads Inn, B & B, US 29S, 293-6382
Econo Lodge, 400 Emmet St., 296-2104
   2014 Holdiay Drive, 295-3185
English Inn, B & B, 2000 Morton Dr., 971-9900
English Inn Guest House, 316 14th St. NW, 295-7707
   Guest house Reservations Svc. 979-7264 or 979-8327
Holiday Inn North, US 29N, 293-9111
Holiday Inn South, I-64, 5th St., Ex., 977-5100
Hollymead Inn, 3001 Hollymead Dr., 973-8488
Howard Johnson's, 13th & W. Main, 296-8121
Ivy Motor Court, Ivy, US 250W, 293-3096
Overlook Motel, US 250E, 293-9154
Quality Inn, US 250E, 977-3300
Ramada Inn, US 29N, 977-7700
Town & Country Motor Lodge, US 250E, 293-6191
University Lodge Motel, 140 Emmet St., 293-5141
White House Motel, US 250E, 977-7227
Big Meadows Lodge, Skyline Dr., 703/999-2221
Graves Mountain Lodge, Syria, 923-4231
Prospect Hill Inn, Trevilians, 703/967-0844
Skyland Lodge, Skyline Dr.,703/999-2211
Wintergreen Resort, Wintergreen, 325-2200

Camping
Cambrae Lodge KOA, 296-9881
Lake Reynovia, 296-1910
Montfair Resort/Farm, 823-5202
Monticello-Skyline Safari, 703/456-5409

HISTORY:
No attempt will be made to tell the story of this community. To do so would be presumptuous. The history of this nation's early beginning is so closely entwined with the Charlottesville story. Certainly, this is where so much of American history got its foundation.

Queen Charlotte of England gave her name to the city which was established in 1762 from the surrounding wilderness. Virginia has often been referred to as the "Mother of Presidents." Yet, it was here in Charlottesville that, at one time or another, many of these distinguished Americans lived: James Monroe, James Madison, and Thomas Jefferson. These were the men that played an important part in establishing the tradition that we in America know and enjoy today. Surely, they played a key part in the formulation of today's Charlottesville.

UNIVERSITY OF VIRGINIA
One of the prime movers for this great University was Thomas Jefferson when Central College was chartered. Funds were raised

from all over the state. In 1819 the University of Virginia was formally chartered. Mr. Jefferson was appointed to the Board of Visitors and as presiding officer he was given the title of "Rector." These were the people that governed the affairs of the University.

So much of the architecture and general planning are directly attributed to Jefferson. He was very much a person of creative genius. It is so interesting to realize that he was almost 80 years old when this miracle of grace and beauty was designed.

The first class of students was received by the University in 1825 with the admission of 68 students.

The Rotunda, the Lawn, the surrounding buildings, and its gardens must be seen to be appreciated. The Rotunda is open daily between 9:00 AM and 4:45 PM. Tours may be arranged by appointment by calling 804/924-1019.

The University of Virginia, known locally as UVA has an enrollment of about 17,000. The College of Arts and Sciences is the largest. The University is well known for its law and medical schools as well as commerce and business administration. Among its disciplines are engineering, architecture, and education. This is an institution that excels in many fields and has been so acknowledged on both national and world-wide levels.

The medical school has played a great part in the establishment of Charlottesville as a regional medical center. Even today, as this is being written, plans are well under way to expand the medical facilities at the University Hospital.

Athletics plays an important role in University life today. The University of Virginia, a member of the Atlantic Coast Conference, has been exceedingly successful in basketball during recent years, being numbered among the nation's best. A recent distinguished graduate of the university, a native of Harrisonburg, Ralph Sampson, played a big part in that accomplishment.

Over the years countless well known persons in the life of this nation have attended this school. From the early era, 1826 to be exact, we would cite as an example, Edgar Allan Poe.

Charlottesville is very much a college town in every sense. The impact on the community can not be minimized. This is especially noted when one realizes that of an area work force of 63,000 persons more than 9000 are in the employ of the university.

SIGHTSEEING

Your adventure to this very interesting and colorful area could well commence at the Visitors Bureau. This agency is a cooperative effort of various governmental and business agencies. This is the ideal place to commence your enjoyable visit.

MONTICELLO — Undoubtedly one of the area's top tourist attractions is the homeplace of Thomas Jefferson. You are cautioned to remember that local residents refer to the former owner as "Mr." Jefferson. You are also advised to give the Italian "twist" to the homeplace, MONT-ih-CHEL-O. Now, you are ready to embark on a knowledgeable visit to the yesteryear surroundings of this very remarkable man. This home was very much the man as he was forever designing and re-designing. The beauty and innovativeness must be noted. On the latter, Jefferson was eons ahead of his time. Open daily; admission charge.

CASTLE HILL — This home built by Dr. Thomas Walker in 1765 is an ideal example of gracious colonial living. This residence has been visited by a succession of prominent American statesmen. Open daily; admission charge.

ASH LAWN — The residence of President James M̶a̶d̶i̶s̶o̶n̶ *Monroe* is a home museum. The visitor is given the opportunity to visualize the plantation life of the 19th century at first hand. Open daily; admission charge.

MICHIE TAVERN MUSEUM — This famed eating place of yester-year found such personages as Madison, Monroe, and Lafayette as dinner customers. Here is an opportunity to learn more about the entertainment that the early colonials enjoyed. Open daily, admission charge. You can also have an opportunity to dine at the "Ordinary" which is open from 11:30 AM until 3:00 PM.

UNIVERSITY OF VIRGINIA — This was discussed earlier.

HISTORIC DOWNTOWN CHARLOTTESVILLE — We suggest a walking tour which is a stroll back in time. This area will include three streets; it covers some six blocks. There are numerous examples of buildings depicting the varying periods of Charlottesville life. Included are examples of early and mid 19th Century construction. This historic neighborhood is adjacent to a recently constructed Mall. Today and yesterday are blended together so pleasantly. The area becomes an oasis free of automobiles. A wonderful opportunity to browse and shop enhances the walking experience.

COUNTRYSIDING:

There is so much of beauty that one can behold in the surrounding countryside. Undoubtedly, this is the reason that so many professionals from the northeast and the midwest have invested in property in this region. Naturally, the new found oil money has also infiltrated into the real estate economy.

Why not steal some time from your formalized sightseeing to explore the countryside. We are confident that you will discover something of either restful tranquility or spectacular awesomeness. Let us think of one possibility that we found quaint and quiet and totally away from it all. We drove north on US 29 to Madison where we branched off on Va. 231 and thence Va. 670 past a sleepy hamlet called Syria. No, we didn't find any Arabs here. What we found was the rural America that had to exist many years ago. We found beautiful rolling countryside. We found the coolness that exists when we are in the forest with a stream that runs over rocks. The sound of moving water. The altitude is getting higher and we are just beyond the boundaries of the Shenandoah National Park. Nestled among this piece of tranquility was a rustic but modern resort, Graves Mountain Lodge.

Undoubtedly, one of the most beautiful options available is the trip to the west which can be taken on either I-64 or US 250 to Afton and the spectacular overview that one finds at Rockfish Gap. At Afton Mountain there are numerous options. You might want to go into the National Park and the Skyline Drive or in the opposite direction taking the Blue Ridge Parkway. Both ways you are treated to controlled beauty.

You might consider another option and that would be to remain on I-64 and get off at Exit 17. You are now on US 340 and heading towards Stuarts Draft. Wander on some of the smaller roads that branch off US 340 and gaze at the neat and well organized farms. Many of them are owned by the hard working Mennonites that are concentrated in the area. This is a wonderful opportunity to marvel upon hard working people that dedicate their lives to the highest principles known to man. It is a wonderful thing to reflect upon the successful and fruitful farmland that they have nurtured.

There are still more options available to the explorer. Between Waynesboro and Charlottesville, after having traversed a part of Albemarle County, you are in Nelson County. This is a county that is blessed with spectacular scenery for its 11,700 citizens. The inhabitants are scattered throughout the County. About ¾ of the county is forested. The terrain ranges from rolling hills to more pronounced mountains. A visit to Crabtree Falls, said to be the highest waterfall east of the Mississippi — it descends a 1500 foot mountainside in a series of beautiful falls. Trails may be found throughout the mountain area. The Appalachian Trail runs through the county. Bear, deer, and small game are plentiful and are hunted during season. The fisherman has the Tye, Piney, Rockfish, and James Rivers.

All that we attempt to do on these pages is offer suggestions. The actual development of the idea should come from you. Don't be afraid to wander up a strange by-way. It could prove to be the highpoint of your trip. If perchance it is just a dead end — well, then — try another trail.

Education
Piedmont Virginia Community College is a two year college and part of the Virginia Community College System. Enrollment runs about 3350 students. Miller School is a highly regarded preparatory school for boys. Oakland School is a residential and day school with summer program for children with learning disabilities from 9 to 16. Contact 804/293-9059.

SPECTATOR SPORTS — Since this is a university community, there is a full schedule of intercollegiate contests in most major and minor sports.

Cultural
Art, music, theater possibilities are limitless. We would suggest that you contact the local Visitor's Center or Chamber of Commerce for up to date information.

Annual Events
The Dogwood Festival - Mid - April.
Historic Garden Week - Last week in April.
Thanksgiving Hunt Weekend - Thanksgiving season.
Christmas in Charlottesville - Christmas season.

Specific information on the above and other events may be secured from the Chamber of Commerce: 804/295-3141.

CHARLOTTESVILLE
Geography
The city is situated 110 miles southwest of Washington, and approximately 70 miles from Richmond. The distance from Roanoke is 115 miles. Contiguous to Charlottesville is Albemarle County.

Population
This is a university community that expands during the school year and diminishes during the summer months. The year round base runs about 40,000 people. Albemarle County is about 57,000. This is

a very sophisticated and cosmopolitan region. Principal industries are education, manufacturing, retailing, medicine, hi-tech, and travel.

Transportation & Logistics

The Charlottesville-Albemarle Airport is located approximately nine miles north of the city on US 29. It is served by Piedmont Airlines which offers trunk service. Commuter service is provided by Air Virginia and Henson Airlines. The latter was recently purchased by Piedmont Airlines.

AMTRAK & BUS — Rail service is provided by Norfolk & Southern as well as AMTRAK. Trailways furnishes the bus service.

CLIMATE — The community enjoys four seasons with the full range of temperature. There will be some snowfall during the colder months. During the summer one notices a certain amount of humidity.

Topography

The elevation is about 850 feet and the community ranges from hilly to rolling countryside. As you drive to the west towards Augusta County on either I-64 or US 250 you will climb to higher elevations. It will be here that you enter the Blue Ridge and an immediate change in temperature and humidity can be noted. The altitude will climb to about 2500 feet.

INVASION ROUTE NORTH —
WESTERN VIRGINIA IN THE CIVIL WAR

By George E. Beetham, Jr.

They stood waiting in the freezing mist — once proud veterans who had faced the best the North could send against them.

Time, money, manpower, and industrial strength were the odds they could not beat. Four long years of bitter warfare had wiped out the gains of battles won through brilliant generalship, hard marching, and tenacious fighting.

The place was a low ridge just west of the Shenandoah Valley town of Waynesboro, Virginia, where they stood to dispute passage by Maj. Gen. Philip Henry Sheridan's blue-clad troops to gaps in the Blue Ridge behind them. They were officially Wharton's Division of the Army of Northern Virginia's Second Corps, led by Lt. Gen. Jubal Anderson Early.

Early's men faced an impossible task that day — March 2, 1865. They were a military unit in name only. Their numbers reduced by fighting, they had spent the winter near Fishersville to the west, consuming precious food supplies.

The northern troops that attacked them were under the command of Brig. Gen. George Armstrong Custer — then a rising and aggressive cavalry commander.

Custer had some of his troops dismount for a flank attack and sent a mounted cavalry charge head-on through the middle of town.

The Confederate line broke — men died in the freezing rain and others were wounded. Almost everybody else was rounded up and marched off as prisoners of war — just about a month before the surrender at Appomattox. It perhaps demonstrates what the war had become that none of the Confederates captured that day attempted to escape while being marched to prison camps in the north — even though a Southern cavalry force attacked their captors and gave them an opportunity.

*****

The first pitched battle of the Civil War took place on the plains of Manassas. The end came at Appomattox. The Piedmont Plain of Virginia was the scene of heavy fighting as the North's Army of the Potomac battled the South's Army of Northern Virginia over routes to the capital cities of Washington, D.C., and Richmond.

But the Blue Ridge Mountains and the Shenandoah Valley figured into the fighting early in the war and remained a strategic factor right up until the lopsided Battle of Waynesboro.

When the war opened, Thomas Jonathon Jackson was an artillery professor at Virginia Military Institute in Lexington, Va. Jackson was commissioned a colonel in the Virginia Militia and sent to Harpers Ferry where he was put in command of a force.

He etched his name in history as a brigadier general at Manassas when his troops turned back a Northern assault. They called him Stonewall after that.

Jackson was the Southern general who put the Shenandoah Valley to good strategic use — force marching his troops up and down the Valley in his 1862 campaign that resulted in defeat of four federal forces.

The Confederate general realized that the presence of his troops in the Valley would tie up federal units that otherwise might have been sent to reinforce the Army of the Potomac under Maj. Gen. George B. McClellan in his campaign to take Richmond.

Jackson, after delivering stunning blows to Northern forces in the Valley, marched eastward to participate in the battles that repulsed McClellan's assault. He rose to lieutenant general before his death at Chancellorsville.

During his Valley Campaign, Jackson defeated a northern force under Brig. Gen. Robert H. Milroy near McDowell — west of Staunton. He then marched to Front Royal to take a federal garrison there by surprise and defeated still another Northern force near Winchester.

Quickly, he led his troops toward Harpers Ferry, bluffing an attack on the federal garrison there. This created panic in the federal government. There were no other forces between Jackson and Washington.

But northern generals were reacting to the threat, and Jackson knew this. A force under Maj. Gen. John C. Fremont was moving eastward from the Alleghany Mountains while a force under Maj. Gen. Irvin McDowell was moving into the Valley from the east.

They hoped to trap Jackson in a pincer movement, or to cut his supply line.

Jackson raced southward, slipping through the closing jaws of the pincer, and retreated up the Valley to the west of Massanutten Mountain, which divides the Shenandoah between Strasburg and Harrisonburg.

At the tiny village of Cross Keys, Jackson turned on the leading troops of Fremont. After defeating them, he turned east and beat the advance of McDowell's force near Port Republic. The northern generals backed off, and as Jackson marched east to Richmond, they sent back reports that he was still in the Valley.

*****

Jackson's campaign did two things. It showed that geography can play a part in military strategy, and it demonstrated that the Shenandoah Valley was a natural invasion route pointed at the heart of the north.

Screened from the Piedmont Plain by the Blue Ridge, the Valley pointed northeastward at the cities of Philadelphia, Baltimore, and Washington itself.

This bit of geographic happenstance was put to use during Gen. Robert E. Lee's Gettysburg Campaign. Lee successfully moved his three corps down the Valley, using cavalry to block the Blue Ridge gaps and screen his movement from the prying eyes of northern cavalry.

Federal forces were unable to pinpoint the location of the invading Confederates, and the result was panic and confusion in northern cities.

After the northern victory at Gettysburg, the war shifted to the east as Lee shifted his army between Culpeper and Northern Virginia. By the early part of 1864, Lt. Gen. Ulysses S. Grant was put in command of all Union armies, bringing with him a plan for the defeat of the South.

That plan would work eventually, but it took a year of fighting for it to unfold. Part of the plan would be destruction of the Shenandoah Valley as a strategic factor that the South could use at will.

Gen. Early had, by 1864, risen to the command of Jackson's old corps and cleared the Valley of all federal forces. He marched over the same route that Jackson and Lee had used, and advanced all the way to the outskirts of Washington. But he lacked the strength to take the federal capital and retreated.

Grant then assigned to Sheridan the task of destroying Early's force, and the Shenandoah Valley as well. Besides its value as an invasion route, the Valley provided farm products to feed the Confederacy. Grant told Sheridan to capture livestock and destroy any produce that couldn't be carried off.

Sheridan defeated Early at Winchester, again later at Cedar Creek after his famous ride from Winchester to rally his troops.

The piecemeal destruction of Early's forces followed, as did burning of Valley farms. The work of destroying the Valley was complete by the time Early's few remaining men stood in the freezing mist outside of Waynesboro.

The Confederacy fell a month later when Lee surrendered at Appomattox. But Civil War history still remains to be discovered in the rolling hills and mountains of Western Virginia. Near New Market is the site of the charge of Virginia Military Institute cadets against the federal troops of Maj. Gen. Franz Sigel — still revered in VMI tradition.

*****

Much of the Valley remains virtually unchanged from the days more than a hundred years ago when marching armies made history. Where Stonewall's men made their way along the dusty Valley Pike, modern U.S. 11 and Interstate 81 now offer an afternoon's review of their campaigns.

Museums, historical markers, and the Hall of Valor at New Market Battlefield help bring those days back to life for anyone who wants to experience a glimpse into the nation's history.

Farms and ante-bellum houses still remain in the Valley — the guns long since have been silenced and put to rest.

George E. Beetham, Jr., is a Philadelphia, Pa., native who has been adopted by Virginia. He is a reporter for The News-Virginian in Waynesboro, Va., and has contributed to Appalachian Trailway News.

— Virginia State Travel Service
Raven's Roost, Blue Ridge Parkway

HARRISONBURG

Lodgings: (703)
Belle Meade Red Carpet Inn, I-81, Ex. 62, 434-6704
Coachman Inn Motel & Rest., I-81, Ex. 65, 434-5301
Econo Lodge, I-81, Ex. 64, 433-2576
Elkton Motel, US 33, Elkton, 298-1463
Holiday Inn, I-81, Ex. 62, 434-9981
Howard Johnson's Motor Lodge, I-81, Ex. 63, 434-6671
Marvilla Motel, I-81, Ex. 64, 433-3687
Massanutten Village Resort Hotel, I-81, Ex. 64E, 289-9441
Rebel's Roost Motel, I-81, Ex. 62, 434-9696
Rockingham Motel, I-81, Ex. 62, 433-2588
Sheraton Inn, I-81, Ex. 64E, 433-2521
The Village Inn, I-81, Ex. 61-62, 434-7355
Best Western, I-81, Ex. 69, Mt. Jackson, 477-2911
Bryce Resort, Bayse, I-81, Ex. 69, 856-212
Sky Chalet Country Inn, Bayse, I-81, Ex. 69, 856-2147

Campgrounds:
Swift Run Campground, 298-8086

Dining:
Belle Meade Rest. & Lounge, US 11S, 434-2367
Candlelight Inn, 317 N. Main, Bridgewater, 828-6776
Capt. Graham's Seafood Rest., 885 E. Market, 434-4023
China Inn, 68 Carlton St., 433-9595
Christopher's, 51 Court Square, 433-9457
Dutch Pantry, 1005 E. Market St., 434-9808
Golden China Restaurant, 30 W. Water St., 434-1285
Holiday Inn Voyager Rest., US 11S, 434-0823
Jo's Restaurant, 68 W. Water St., 433-9146
Kettle Room Restaurant, Rte. 644, 13 mi. E., 289-9441
Lloyd's Steak House, US 11S, 434-9843
Sheraton Inn Olympic Room Rest., I-81, Ex. 64E, 433-2521
Coachman Inn Restaurant, I-81, Ex. 65, 434-5301
Fiesta Cantina, I-81, Ex. 64E. 434-0550
Golden Corral Family Steak House, 1580 S. Main, 433-8680
Heritage Family Restaurant, 350 Waterman Dr., 433-3911
Howard Johnson's Restaurant, I-81, Ex. 63, 434-2455
J.M.'s Pub & Deli, 1007 S. Main, 433-8537
Mosby's Mill, 20 W. Mosby Rd., 434-6243
Ole Virginia Ham Cafe, 85 W. Market, 434-6572
Shoney's, I-81, Ex. 64, 434-2626
Village Inn Restaurant, US 11S, 434-7355
Western Steer Family Steak House, US 33E, 434-5775
Woody's Restaurant, 101 N. Main, Bridgewater, 828-3002
Donut Man, Rte. 33E, 434-6404

Calhoun's Fine Food & Drink Est. 1983

Dine With Us During Your Visit. You'll Enjoy Our Fine Dinner Menu.

51 Court Square PHONE 434-4464 FOR RESERVATIONS

Ice Cream Factory, Valley Mall, 433-8381
Kentucky Fried Chicken Rest., 891 Cantrell Ave., 433-8464
L & S Diner, 255 N. Liberty, 434-5572
McDonald's, Carlton St., 434-0055
Roman Delight, Valley Mall, 433-8388
Roy Rogers Family Restaurant, 1570 E. Market, 434-4194
Scotland Yard, US 11S, 433-1113
Tastee Freez, US 240, Grottoes, 249-4817
Wendy's, US 33E, 434-3368

Sightseeing:
History buffs will find that a very good place to start is at 301 S. Main Street where the Harrisonburg-Rockingham Historical Society Museum is located (434-4762). Admission and parking are free. Visitors will find a library, archives, photo collections, exhibits, and Civil War artifacts just to mention a portion of what is contained. A historical research service is available as well as a book shop.

MASSANUTTEN CAVERNS — There are no steps in this wonderland located a short distance east of Harrisonburg. Take US 33 to Va. 620 — your reference point is Keezletown. The caverns are open from June until Labor Day. Contact: 703/999-2266.

GRAND CAVERNS — Get off I-81 at Exit 60 and proceed to Grottoes and you will soon be at these caverns. This is a spectacular underworld vista. The caverns are located within the Grand Caverns Regional Park.

DANIEL HARRISON HOUSE — Built around 1749 by Daniel Harrison, a brother of Harrionburg's founder, Thomas Harrison. The house is located just north of Dayton, a town in the southwestern part of the county. It's open to the public on Fridays, Saturdays, Sundays from 1:30 PM to 4:00 PM. Contact: Fort Harrison, Inc. P.O. Box 366, Dayton, VA 22821; 703/434-4762.

NATURAL CHIMNEYS — This attraction is located at Mount Solon and you would depart I-81 at Exit 61. It is here that the towering chimneys go up 120 feet in the air. A unique sight that justifies the trip. It is here that the annual Natural Chimneys Jousting Tournament is held. It was first held in 1821 and is purported to be the oldest continuously held sporting event in America. It is held annually on the third Saturday of August.

Education

Harrisonburg and the immediate environs are blessed with some very fine institutions of higher learning. Two of them are located within the city limits of Harrisonburg.

JAMES MADISON UNIVERSITY — Established by the Virginia General Assembly in 1908 as the State Normal and Industrial School for Women. It opened its doors in 1909 with an enrollment of 209 women and a faculty of 15. It became a state teachers college in 1924 and remained as such until 1938 when it was renamed Madison College.

The college became fully coeducational in 1966 and its status to a university became official in 1977 when it assumed its present name. The current enrollment of approximately 9000 comes from all over the state. There is a very heavy concentration of out of state students from the surrounding northeastern states.

On the undergraduate level there are bachelor degree programs offered in countless areas encompassing such fields as education, computer science, business management, economics, language arts, data processing, music, and communication arts. Those are just some of the many areas. Offerings for Master degree programs are increasing in enrollment and popularity each year.

This beautiful campus tastefully blends the old with the new. "Up Campus" is an example of ivy covered blue stone buildings dating back to the turn of the century. "The Village" and the "Lake Dorms" are of modern multistory brick design. Included on this attractive campus are its modern indoor and outdoor sports facilities. For further information contact: James Madison University, Harrisonburg, VA 22807; 703/433-6211.

BRIDGEWATER COLLEGE — Affiliated with the Church of the Brethren this four year liberal arts college is located at nearby Bridgewater, Virginia. It was founded in 1880. Current enrollment census will run approximately 900. Located on the campus is the Pritchett Museum containing more than 5000 artifacts. It is open to the public.

EASTERN MENNONITE COLLEGE — This church related college with a student body of approximately 950 students was estab-

lished in 1917. This institution provides a full liberal arts curriculum. The science building has a planetarium and museum that is open to the public on Sundays.

BLUE RIDGE COMMUNITY COLLEGE — This two year institution with an enrollment in excess of 2000 is located in Weyers Cave, Virginia. It is a member school of the state Community College system. This institution serves the cities of Harrisonburg, Staunton, and Waynesboro as well as the counties of Augusta and Rockingham.

History
This area is one of the principal turkey raising centers of the world. Harrisonburg is considered as a regional shopping center for the surrounding Rockingham County residents as well as those from nearby West Virginia. Harrisonburg was originally named Rocktown because of the limestone in the area. In the year 1779, one Thomas Harrison donated 2½ acres for the county courthouse that is located in the city's center.

Local legend tells of Harrison and a Mr. Keezel, for whom the nearby town of Keezletown was named, racing by horseback to Richmond. Each was headed to the state capital for the purpose of filing his town as the county seat for Rockingham County. It is reported that Harrison won the race. Thus, we have the story of how the county seat derived its name and place.

Geography

Harrisonburg can be reached on I-81 at an elevation of 1320 feet. It is some 124 miles from Washington; 116 miles from Richmond; and the distance from Roanoke is 111 miles. The city serves as a shopping center for surrounding Rockingham County residents as well as those from nearby West Virginia. This region is regarded as one of the top turkey producing centers of the world. There are numerous industries in the surrounding area. The Blue Ridge Mountains are on the east and the Alleghanies on the west.

Population

The population for this city will run about 20,000. Rockingham County will stand at an approximate 57,000.

Climate

The strength of agriculture attests to the well balanced climate of the region. There are four seasons here with several days of snow during the winter. As true of other communities of the region there will be some days of 90 degree temperature during the summer.

Transportation

The Shenandoah Valley Airport at Weyers Cave, some 15 miles away, serves this area along with the cities of Staunton, Waynes-

— George Beetham

Sheep & Lambs, Highland County

boro, and the County of Augusta. Henson Airlines, a commuter service recently purchased by Piedmont Airlines, provides connecting air service to connecting airline hub cities. Persons wishing to come to Harrisonburg can use such hub points as Washington, Baltimore, and currently Pittsburgh. Hub cities vary with the whims of marketers for interested airlines. Service into such cities as Charlottesville, Roanoke, Richmond, and Washington can be considered as an alternate. The Bridgewater Air Park can accomodate smaller private aircraft. Bus and nearby train service is also available to the community.

ORANGE

Campgrounds: (703)
Beaver Run Campgrounds, Gordonsville, 832-2844
Bud-Lea Campground, Madison, 948-4186
Christopher Run Campground, Mineral, 894-4744
Lake Anna Family Campground, Mineral, 894-5529
Mountain Springs Campground, Syria, 923-4229
Small Country, VA, Louisa, 967-2431

Dining: (703)
Horsefeathers, 322 Madison Rd., 672-2666
McDonald's, 153 Madison Rd., 672-2422
Orange Gourmet, 182 Byrd St., 672-3514

Potpourri
Orange County is a very historical and very beautiful section of the state. It was named for William IV, Prince of Orange and Anne, Princess Royal of England. The county was formed in 1734. It was the original site of an early colony of Germans who were brought here by Governor Alexander Spotswood commencing in 1714 to defend the western frontier and to mine iron.

The Town of Orange got its start in the 1750's. Nearby Gordonsville was named for Nathaniel Gordon, who opened a tavern in 1787 to serve western travelers that crossed the Blue Ridge.

This entire region boasts as a very wealthy storehouse of the American experience. Montpelier, the home of James Madison, is located west of the town of Montpelier. Virginia 20 and 231 pass the estate which can be viewed from the road. Born in 1784 near Barboursville was Zachary Taylor, the 12th President of the United States.

During the Civil War this was a region that found itself in the midst of numerous campaigns.

Sightseeing:
CHANCELLORSVILLE BATTLEFIELD — This important battle locale during the Civil War has been maintained by the National Park Service and is located at the intersection of Va. 20 and Va. 3 some 14 miles form I-95.

GERMANNA COMMUNITY COLLEGE — The library contains extensive collections of books and documents pertaining to the early settlement.

WILDERNESS BATTLEFIELD — This is also maintained by the National Park Service and was the site of the confrontation between Lee and Grant on May 4, 1864. Located on Va. 20 en route to Orange.

JAMES MADISON MUSEUM & INFORMATION CENTER —129 Caroline St., Orange. This commemorates the period of James Madison as well as his interest in the Constitution and in agrarian reform.

ST. THOMAS CHURCH — Located at 119 Caroline St. — on the National register of Historic Places. The church reflects the design of Thomas Jefferson. It has two Tiffany windows and contains the original pew used by Lee during the winter of 1863.

ORANGE COUNTY COURTHOUSE — Located on Main Street, this building dates back to 1858. It contains records dating back to 1734 and includes the wills of Governor Spotswood and James Madison. It is on the National Register of Historic Places.

THE RESIDENCE — Woodberry Forest School is of Jeffersonian architecture and open during school the term — on the National Register of Historic Places.

MAYHURST — Take Va. 15 to Gordonsville. Built in 1859 you may drive past the former headquarters of Civil War General A. P. Hill — on the National Register of Historic Places.

WOODLEY — Built in the 1780's. This estate is the home of Ambrose, brother of James Madison. You may see this from the road.

MONTPELIER — Home of James Madison located on Va. 20 to Va. 231. It may be viewed from the road. However, it is not open to the public. It is a National Historic Landmark.

MADISON FAMILY CEMETERY — James and Dolly Madison are buried here. It is open the year round and may be approached by turning at Rt. 639.

EXCHANGE HOTEL — Located in the Town of Gordonsville; it is currently being restored. This was used as a receiving hospital by the Confederate Army during the Civil War — on the National Register of Historic Places.

MAIN STREET — Bordered by examples of Victorian architecture.

MAPLEWOOD CEMETERY — Rt. 33 west of Gordonsville. There are Confederate graves here — no markers.

MONTEBELLO — Va. 33 to US 29. From the road you can see the traditional birthplace of Zachary Taylor.

BARBOURSVILLE — Excepting Sundays, it is open to the public with a day's notice. It was the home of Governor James Barbour and is now the site of a vineyard — on the National Register of Historic Places.

ORANGE COUNTY CHAMBER OF COMMERCE — For further information they may be reached at 703/672-5216 or by writing them at: 129 Caroline St., Orange, VA 22960. Make certain that you ask them for the excellent folder entitled "Orange County Virginia—in the Middle of History." This very well organized folder lists sightseeing highlights with a coded map that points out the highlights for you.

Geography

The county ranges from fairly steep, to rolling hills, to level. Elevation varies from 200 feet to 1200 feet. There are four seasons during the year with both hot summer and cold winter days. Snowfall will hit about 17 inches while rainfall will be around 42 inches. The county is tied into US 250, US 29, I-64, and I-95. US 15 is the primary north-south highway. US 522 and 33 as well as Va. 3, 20, 231 serve the county. Route 3 is a four lane arterial highway. Population for the county is approximately 19,000 persons. The Town of Orange, the county seat, is 32 miles from Charlottesville; 72 from Richmond and 87 from Washington, D.C. The setting here is rural and ranks among the most beautiful in the state.

In addition to the two airports within the county serving small aircraft, there is commercial air service provided at the Charlottesville Airport some 25 miles away and the Washington area airports to the north. In addition, there is local rail and bus service.

— Virginia Division of Tourism
Thanksgiving Hunt Weekend, Charlottesville

STAUNTON

Lodgings: (703)

Bel-Grae Inn, 515 West Frederick St., 886-5151
Holiday Inn-Downtown, 268 N. Central Ave., 886-3401
Holiday Inn-North, I-81, Ex. 58, 885-5111
Stonewall Jackson Hotel, 28 S. Market, 885-1581
Armstrong's Motel, I-81, Ex. 55A, 337-2611
Augusta Motor Court, Mt. Sidney, I-81, Ex. 58 S & 59 N, 248-8040
Day's Inn, I-81, Ex. 55A, 337-3031
Douglas Arms Motor Court, Greenville, I-81, Ex. 55, 337-2511
Econo Lodge-Countryside Inn, Verona, I-81, Ex. 59, 248-8981
Econo Travel, I-81, Ex. 57, 885-5158
Hessian House, I-81, Ex. 55, 337-1231
Ingleside Red Carpet Inn, I-81, Ex. 58, 885-1201
Master Host Motel, I-81, Ex. 58, 885-0377

Campgrounds

Sherando Lake, 942-5965
Monticello Skyline Safari, 456-6409
Natural Chimneys Reg. Park. 350-2510
Rhema Lake Camping Resort, 337-1779
Shenandoah Acres Resort, 337-1911
Walnut Hills Campgrounds, 337-9773

Dining

Buckhorn Inn, US 250, Churchville, 885-2900
China Gate Restaurant, 11 W. Johnson St., 886-6792
Ingleside Red Carpet, I-81, Ex. 57, 885-1201
McCormick's Pub & Restaurant, 41 N. Augusta, 885-3111
Legend, 501 Thornrose Ave., 886-4220
White Star Mills, 1 Mill St., 885-3409
Stonewall Jackson Hotel, 28 S. Market, 885-1581
Arena Restaurant & Lounge, Rt. 254W, 885-6555
Armstrong's Restaurant, I-81, Ex. 55A, 337-2611
Angus Steak House, 2302 W. Beverley, 886-9833
Beverley Restaurant, 12 E. Beverley St., 886-4317
Beverley Restaurant North, 2215 N. Augusta, 885-7585
Brooks Restaurant, Verona, US 11 N, 248-1722
Farmstead, Verona, US 11 N, 885-8013
Golden Corral, 1000 Greenville Ave., 885-8698
Holiday Inn-Downtown, 268 N. Central, 886-3401
Holiday Inn-North, I-81, Ex. 58, 885-5111
Howard Johnson's, Greenville, I-81, 337-2844
Our Place, Swoope, Rt. 254 W, 885-7515
Rowe's Family Restaurant, I-81 & I-64, 886-1833
Shoney's, I-81 & US 250
Harry's Lunch, 909 Greenville Ave., 886-9815

Wong's, 812 Spring Hill Rd., 886-6955
Pampered Palate, 26 E. Beverley, 885-0601
Tack Room, 12 N. Central, 885-4200
WRS Cafeteria, Staunton Plaza, US 11 S, l885-1072
Wright's Dairy Rite, 346 Greenville Ave., 886-0435
Bonanza, 906 Greenville, 885-5971
Brother's Pizza, Staunton Plaza, US 11 S, 885-8787
Burger King, 1001 Greenville, 885-5925
Caretti's Pizza, 638 Greenville, 885-7821
Donut King, 837 Greenville, 885-4143
Hardee's, 241 N. Central, 885-5767
Kentucky Fried Chicken, 838 Greenville, 886-5619
Long John Silver's, 641 Greenville, 885-0050
McDonald's, 910 Greenville, 885-1170
Pizza Hut, 704 N. Coalter, 885-8875
   835 Greenville, 885-8816
Pizza Inn, 703 Greenville, 885-8103
Tastee Freez, 2207 W. Beverley, 885-0049
Wendy's, 703 Greenville, 885-5250
Burger House, Verona, US 11 N, 248-8214
Kentucky Fried Chicken, Verona, US 11 N, 885-7795
Peck's Barbecue, Fishersville, US 250 E, 885-7000

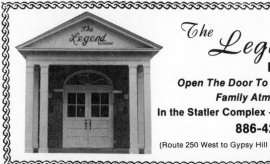

History

The city dates back to the year 1749. It is well to know that it is pronounced similar to the word "stand" — so, you would say STANTON. You spell it S-T-A-U-N-T-O-N but pronounce it the other way. The original 25 acres of land was owned by Sir William Beverley. The city, itself, was named after Lady Staunton who was wife of William Gooch, a colonial governor of Virginia. It was in 1732 that John Lewis brought a group of Scotch-Irish settlers to the immediate area.

The area that surrounds Staunton is Augusta County. It was formed in 1738. Augusta was named "Mother of Counties." From this territory most of the counties west of the Blue Ridge, nearly all of West Virginia's counties, and the entire states of Kentucky, Ohio, Indiana, and Illinois were formed.

There has always existed a close relationship between city and county. Even today, it is very much a county seat type community. It is of germane interest to note that extensive merger-consolidation negotiations are currently taking place between the two political entities. This will result in the re-writing of the maps and the changing of many vital statistics. Currently, the population for Staunton is about 21,000.

It is to be noted that in 1781 Staunton served as the capitol of the Commonwealth of Virginia. Not only was it important in the Colonial era but it served as a very important hub during the Civil War.

The City Manager form of government got its start in this city in the year 1908. One can easily see that this city steeped in history with its preserved architecture and its people of solid conservative background have been in the forefront of government reform.

Staunton's most famous son, Woodrow Wilson, was born here on December 28, 1856, while his father served as minister for the First Presbyterian Church.

While on the subject of famed sons, we should make mention of some that are held in very high esteem by residents of this area. The Statler Brothers composed of Harold Reid, Don Reid, Phil Balsley, and Lew Dewitt got their start here and in the surrounding area. They have been showered with countless honors for their down home ballads of grassroots life. A recent illness has caused DeWitt to take an early retirement. His place has been capably replaced, however, by Jimmy Fortune who has been imported to the community. In 1970 the Statler Brothers commenced a tradition that has been continuously repeated each Independence Day since. A celebration known as Happy Birthday USA brings the community together to hear the Statler Brothers perform as well as hearing an additional guest star. In addition, local charitible organizations have an opportunity to earn funds through the operation of concessions. There are games and a host of activities that make this cost free day a highlight of Staunton's year. There is absolutely no admission charge to this event. This past year more than 72,000 persons joined in this tribute to the nation. None of this could have been possible without the impetus that has been enthusiastically given by Staunton's favorite sons.

STONEWALL BRIGADE BAND is the oldest continuously playing municipal band in the United States. It was formed in 1855. Its

Home for the Fourth, Staunton

present name was bestowed upon it by the Confederate States War Department in 1863 during it service in the war. It has been continuously providing musical entertainment since that time. Currently, they play under the bandstand at Gypsy Hill Park on Monday nights during the summer months.

NEWTOWN HISTORIC DISTRICT is a recent addition to the Virginia Landmarks Register. This is the town's oldest continuously occupied residential area, spanning a period of over 150 years. On the east where Newtown adjoins two commercial historic districts, warehouses coexist with elegant brick homes. This creates a strong visual link between traditional downtown and this historic residential neighborhood. Domestic architectural style from the late 18th to the early 20th Centuries are represented. Thornrose Cemetery is included because of its design and the fact they many prominent residents were buried here.

Sightseeing
It is refreshing to walk through a taste of nostalgia and to escape the glass and steel skyscrapers that mark our lifestyle. An interesting walking tour of the downtown treats the visitor to a blend of different eras and different architectural designs. One notes Greek Revival, High Victorian Italianate and Romanesque Revival. Walking through downtown one can commence at Coalter and proceed down Frederick and on to New and over to Beverley to Central and retrace a bit on Beverley back to the start at Coalter. It's about eight blocks round trip and worth the visit back into time.

Your trip should include a visit to the Birthplace of Woodrow Wilson. The charge for admission is quite nominal and well worth the price.

Your walking tour will have you passing the campus of Mary Baldwin College. It sits on a hill and provides a picture postcard sight. It's well worth a picture.

STATLER BROTHERS COMPLEX — A mini museum containing memorabilia and awards received by the Statler Brothers. Daily tours are given at 2:00 PM and a gift shop is located here. For further information: Statler Brothers, 501 Thornrose Ave., Staunton, VA 24401, 703/885-7297.

MONTEREY — A very very scenic driving trip can be taken on US 250 W to Highland County. The distance to Monterey is 45 miles from Staunton and will take approximately 1 hour 15 minutes driving time. The way there is mountainous but the rewards in scenic enjoyment are great. It is very reminiscent of Switzerland. The annual Maple Sugar festival is held in March while the Highland County Fall Foliage Festival is held in October. Specific dates can be secured from the Highland County Chamber of Commerce. Overnight guests can stay at either the Highland Inn or the Montvale Inn. Local businessman George Hooke has built a nine hole golf course that is reported to have greens that do not have to take a back seat to any in the country. A transplanted New York investment broker that we met suggests that an overnight stop in this make believe Swiss village can truly be described as an "ideal overnight oasis stop." Further information: Chamber of Commerce Highland County, Monterey, VA 24465; 703/468-2550.

Educational

MARY BALDWIN COLLEGE — A four-year private college for women, founded in 1842. This school provides a study in liberal arts with opportunities for career preparation. Enrollment runs about 820.

BLUE RIDGE COMMUNITY COLLEGE — Weyers Cave, Virginia.

AUGUSTA MILITARY ACADEMY — Ft. Defiance, Virginia, Boy's prep.

STUART HALL — Girl's prep.

ELIZABETH BRANT SCHOOL OF BUSINESS — Private business.

VIRGINIA SCHOOL FOR THE DEAF & BLIND — State high school.

Recreation
An ideal spot to relax with a picnic basket is the municipally owned Gypsy Hill Park, conveniently located within the city. It's about 400 acres in size and includes ball fields, tennis courts, swimming pool, pond complete with waterfowl, a nine hole golf course, baseball stadium, and football stadium. It is a wonderful place to just stroll and sit.

Golfers have the opportunity to try any of five nearby courses. Skiiers can try the slopes at Massanutten, Wintergreen, Bryce, or the Homestead. Augusta Expo located in nearby Fishersville is a 200 acre complex that from time to time has events of public interest in addition to the annual Fair in July.

STAUNTON BRAVES — A semiprofessional baseball team composed of college players who compete in the regional Valley Baseball League from June to August. It is a good brand of ball that is thoroughly scouted by the major leagues. Numerous major leaguers of note got their start in this league. They play at Moxie Memorial Stadium at Gypsy Hill Park.

Geography & Topography
Staunton is located 150 miles southwest of Washington, D.C. It is 110 miles west of Richmond and 90 miles north of Roanoke. The intersection of I-81 and I-64 make this a strategic hub for travel to East-West and North-South.

The city itself is built on hilly terrain. The surrounding area is heavily involved in agriculture in a very picturesque rolling hilled countryside. The altitude averages around 2000 feet above sea level.

Transportation & Logistics
Air service is provided by Henson Airlines a commuter line which has recently been purchased by Piedmont Airlines. This service operates from Weyers Cave Airport some 15 miles from Staunton. Commuter service is provided to hub citys on the Piedmont system for further connection to Piedmont Airlines scheduled service. Additional air service is available from Woodrum Field, Roanoke, some 90 miles distant. Alternate service is available from Charlottesville some 40 miles away. In Waynesboro there is an airport accommodating charter aircraft.

RAIL — Amtrak

BUS — Greyhound and Trailways.

Population
Staunton approximately 21,000 with surrounding Augusta County at 54,000.

Political Entity
Augusta County and the City of Staunton are in advanced stages of negotiation with prospects of a future consolidation or merger. Terms of the agreement will include provisions as to future name of the locality and the specific form that it will take such as shire or borough. These details should be formulated within the next few years.

The signing of the Federal Reserve Act on display at United Virginia Bank Museum, Staunton.

MANSE TO MUSEUM:
STAUNTON'S WOODROW WILSON BIRTHPLACE

The stately manse at the corner of North Coalter and Frederick Streets watched over Staunton as it grew from a courthouse town to a bustling railroad center in the 1850's to a supply center during the tragic Civil War. It watched the people pull themselves up after the war, and saw the 1890's boom and bust. The Twentieth century dawned, and the pace of life quickened in the town, but changed little in the old manse.

The house, which had served in quiet dignity as families of Presbyterian ministers moved in and out, suddenly took on national importance. One of the many children who had lived in the manse — indeed, one born there — was elected President of the United States.

City leaders, proud of the native son, organized an elaborate celebration to honor Woodrow Wilson. In December, 1912, President-elect Wilson returned to Staunton to celebrate his 56th birthday in the manse where he had entered the world.

From that time on, the manse attracted the curious and the awed who wished to see the President's birthplace. As America's attention shifted from the White House to the battlefields of Europe in "the war to end all wars" then to the peace table at Paris, Staunton's native son with his peace plan was perceived by millions around the world as one of the great leaders of modern history.

That President Wilson's peace program met opposition from European statesmen, and that it was rejected by his own Senate did not diminish his standing as a man of vision and idealism. After his death in 1924, many people hoped to create a suitable memorial to him.

The practice of saving Presidential houses, especially birthplaces, was an early expression of the historic preservation movement in this country. It is not surprising that people thought of preserving President Wilson's birthplace in Staunton.

In 1938, The Woodrow Wilson Birthplace Foundation was chartered "to purchase, preserve, and maintain" the birthplace, together with necessary adjacent property, and "to secure funds for that purpose and for the restoration and permanent endowment thereof."

Shortly after his inauguration to an unprecedented third term in the White House, President Franklin D. Roosevelt came to Staunton in May 1941 to dedicate the Woodrow Wilson Birthplace as a "shrine to freedom." The clouds of a Second World War, so feared by President Wilson when his peace plan was rejected, hung over the United States, and Europe was already plunged into war.

Full time executive directors with graduate training in history and museum administration have been employed to administer the Birthplace according to highest museum standards. The adjacent house on Coalter was converted into administrative offices and a reception center with exhibits and a film for the increasing numbers of visitors coming to the Birthplace. President Wilson's Pierce-Arrow limousine was restored and placed in an exhibit building on the grounds, and the gift shop was expanded to provide more support for museum operations. The Birthplace became one of less than 20% of the museums in the United States to be accredited by the American Association of Museums.

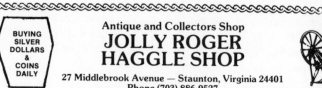

The most exciting development at the Birthplace however, was the restoration project undertaken in 1978. The goal of the trustees was to return the manse to its appearance at the time of President Wilson's birth in 1856. Restoration architect Robert Garbee of Lynchburg conducted extensive architectural and documentary research on the house, and a nationally recognized paint authority did chemical analyses of all interior paints to determine the correct colors for the 1850's. Successful fund-raising by the trustees resulted in major grants from the National Endowment for the Humanities, the Jessie Ball duPont Religious, Charitable, and Educational Fund, and in gifts from numerous generous Staunton and Virginia donors for the restoration. The structural and architectural restoration was completed in 1979, and the reinterpretation of the interior of the manse with appropriate period furnishings and decorations typical of a Presbyterian minister's home in the Shenandoah Valley in the 1850's was completed in 1982.

The emphasis at the Birthplace today is on the expansion of services to tourists and to the local community. The guided tour gives visitors a greater understanding of the family values and lifestyle represented in the manse which did so much to shape the character of this great president. A new exhibit, "Woodrow Wilson: Professor, President, Peacemaker" has been installed in the Reception Center. The film room has been expanded to provide a space for lectures, demonstrations, workshops, and changing exhibits.

An exciting educational program for school-children is being developed, with the help of a federal grant. A trained educator joined the staff to work with administrators and teachers in area public and private schools to prepare educational materials and special programs for students.

The Birthplace is the Staunton area's community museum and looks forward to expanding its usefulness to the community.
 — *Katharine Brown, Ph.D.*
 Executive Director, Woodrow Wilson Birthplace Foundation

WAYNESBORO

Lodgings: (703)
Allstate Motor Court, US 250W, 942-5251
Colony House Motor Lodge, US 250E, 942-4156
Deluxe Motor Court, 2112 W. Main, 949-8253
General Wayne Motor Inn, 620 W. Main, 949-8117
Holiday Inn, US 250E, Afton Mtn., 942-5201
Houff-Heizer Cabin Ct., 1307 W. Main, 949-8123
Red Carpet Inn, US 340 & I-64, 943-1101
Skyline Pkwy. Motor Ct., US 250E, Afton Mtn., 942-1141
Wayne Motor Lodge-Best Western, 640 W. Broad, 942-1171
West Lawn Motel, 2240 W. Main, 942-9551

Campgrounds
Meadow Mtn. Camp Resort, 943-9051
Monticello Skyline Safari, 456-6409
Shenandoah Acres Resort, 337-1191
Waynesboro North 340, 943-9573

Restaurants
Aberdeen Barn, US 250E, Afton Mtn., 949-6334
Apple Crate, 1235 W. Main, 943-0816
Arby's, 204 Rosser Ave., 943-2533
Barbecue King, 2823 W. Main, 949-6226
Bonanza Sirloin Pit, 1501 W. Broad, 949-6353
Broad St. IGA Deli, 1000 W. Broad, 943-8758
Burger King, 1535 W. Broad, 943-2858
Captain's Table, US 250E, Afton, 456-6722
Capt'n Sam's Landing, US 250W, 943-3416
D & W Cafeteria, 2105 W. Main, 943-9362
Ciro's Pizza, 901B Centre-for-Shopping, 942-5169
Dairy Queen, 130 E. Broad, 943-0500
Eatery Ltd., 325 E. Main, 949-6609
Ed's Grill, 1221 E. Main, 949-0225
Four Star Pizza, 141 E. Broad, 943-4545
General Wayne Motor Inn, 620 W. Main, 949-8117
Golden China Restaurant, 1600 E. Main, 943-3323
Golden Corral, W. Main St., 943-6534
Hardee's, 1416 W. Main St., 942-9798
Howard Johnson's, US 250E, Afton Mtn., 943-7211
JR's Pub & Deli, US 250W, 943-6013
Kentucky Fried Chicken, US 340 & I-64, 942-1329
Library Restaurant, 1107 W. Main, 943-7616
Long John Silver's, 1432 W. Main, 943-7475
Luigi's Pizzeria, 141 E. Broad, 943-2323
Lynn's Pancake & Steak, 2120 W. Main, 943-3915
McDonald's, 1501 W. Main, 943-3949

Golden China Restaurant

金 華 酒 家

EXCELLENT CHINESE &
AMERICAN FOOD
FAMILY STYLE—REASONABLE
PRICES — QUICK LUNCH —
SPECIAL DINNERS
• COCKTAILS
• POLYNESIAN DRINKS

- HOURS -
MON - THUR 11 A.M. - 10 P.M.
FRI - SAT 11 A.M. - 11 P.M.
SUN 12:00 NOON - 10 P.M.

TELEPHONE
943-3323

Located on East Main Street toward Afton Mountain

1600 E. MAIN STREET   WAYNESBORO, VIRGINIA

Oriental Restaurant, 250 N. Poplar, 943-7474
Paul's Italian Restaurant, 408 E. Main,m 943-2232
Peking Chinese Restaurant, 2410 W. Main, 943-7149
Pizza Hut, 1412 W. Broad, 943-9092
Pizza Inn, 1441 W. Main, 942-5111
Purple Foot, 1035 W. Broad, 942-9463
Red Carpet Inn, US 340 & I-64, 943-1101
Roma's Italian Restaurant, US 250W
Shoney's, US 340 & I-64, 943-6044
Sub City, 212 W. Main, 943-6260
Tom Boy's, 1220 Broad, 942-1280
Wendy's Family Restaurant, US 250W, 943-7458

Sightseeing
VISITOR CENTER — The Waynesboro Chamber of Commerce
operates a tourist information office in the Skyline Parkway Motor
Court, which is located at the intersection of the Blue Ridge Parkway & Skyline Drive I-64, Exit 19. You may call: 943-5187 or
949-8203.

Waynesboro ideally serves as a hub for day trips in all directions.
Charlottesville by I-64 E. offers numerous opportunities for learning
of the Colonial Virginia of Thomas Jefferson and his contemporar-
ies. If nothing else, the ride on either US 250 or I-64 to Charlottes-

BEST WESTERN
WAYNE MOTOR LODGE, INC.

640 West Broad Street — Waynesboro, Virginia 22980

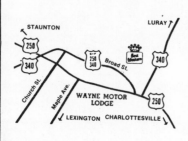

LOCATION: 4 miles from Blue Ridge Parkway and Skyline Drive, on U. S. 250 and 340, 20 miles from Shenandoah Valley Airport, 20 miles from Wintergreen Ski Resort.

61 Units — Individually controlled A/C and Heat Combination Tub and Shower 25 x 50 Ft. Swimming Pool Color Cable TV — Excellent Food — Cocktails

ville justifies the 25 odd miles in each direction. The rolling countryside has real estate price tags of six figure dimensions. We would suggest going over on I-64 and making a stop at one of the scenic overlooks for a breathless sight. Bring your camera. The return trip can be made via parallel but narrower US 250. Refer to the Charlottesville section for sightseeing suggestions.

A second driving possibility from Waynesboro would be a drive in a southerly direction on the Blue Ridge Parkway. This drive would give a good overview of the Rockfish Valley to the east and the Shenandoah Valley to the west. There is a ranger station some five miles or so to the south where a very interesting mountain farm is located. Proceeding further south by another five miles or so is Humpback Rock which would be perfect for a short hike on the Appalachian Trail to the summit. You might check on camping and picnicking in the area.

We would recommend a side trip to Lexington for your consideration. Please refer to that section for further guidance. You might also combine a visit there with one to Natural Bridge.

A visit to Walnut Grove, the home of Cyrus McCormick provides the visitor with an interesting insight into the history of the reaper and the subsequent International Harvester Company. There is a restored grist mill and blacksmith shop. The shade trees, picnic

Real Estate Opportunities in
AUGUSTA COUNTY
at the southern end of the Shenandoah Valley

Bellefonte

Built in the late 1700's and with an interesting history, BELLE-FONTE *is a striking example of classic western frontier architecture. The estate, situated on 12-plus acres, is beautifully restored and well maintained. Mature boxwoods, raised flower beds and an orchard complement the dwelling.*

This estate is but an example of some of the fine homes offered for sale through Barnwell & Jones Realtors, located in the Shenandoah Valley. For brochures and further information on this property or others in the Augusta County area contact our office.

For qualified properties we will consider trade-ins through the ERA "Seller's Security Plan."

P. O. Box 1166
Waynesboro, Virginia 22980
(703) 942-5101 Waynesboro
(703) 885-7811 Staunton

tables, and restroom facilities make this a wonderful stopping point. Walnut Grove is open to the public free of charge seven days a week from eight until five. This is a very worthwhile stop; especially, for those that have an interest in America's agricultural and industrial past.

North from Waynesboro extends the Skyline Drive which travels through the very scenic Shenandoah National Park to Front Royal. This is truly a scenic paradise with much variety. It is not designed for people in a hurry.

SHERANDO LAKE — This is part of the National Forest System. Fishing, boating, camping, and swimming facilities are available.

SHENANDOAH ACRES RESORT — Near Stuarts Draft. This resort is built around a privately owned 3½ acre sand bottom swimming lake. There are picnic and camping facilities, horseback riding, bicycles, hiking, shuffleboard, badminton, and tennis. Contact address is: P.O. Box 308, Stuarts Draft, VA 24477, 337-1911.

Some 12 miles from Waynesboro on US 340 are the Grand Caverns.

North on I-81, you can take in the famed New Market Battlefield Park and combine that with a visit to Shenandoah Caverns or possibly an excursion to Luray Caverns. Natural Chimneys located in Mt. Solon are a curiosity to behold — there are seven towering chimneys.

Close to Waynesboro on the top of Afton Mountain sits the majestic Swannanoa Palace with its formal gardens. There is an admission charge. A fine collection of art abounds, along with the Italian marble and Tiffany glass which contribute to the grandeur of this place.

Baugher Chevrolet-Buick, Inc.

Central Shenandoah Valley's Largest Dealership

An eight-plus acre complex featuring the sale and service of Chevrolet Cars and Trucks and Buick Cars, with service available for most other GM vehicles.

Service Department fully equipped and staffed with GM Trained Technicians.

Large Parts Department, inventory controlled by in-house computer. Overnight UPS.

Under same management for 38 years.

We will always welcome your visit.

BAUGHER CHEVROLET-BUICK, INC.

Highway 250 • P. O. Box 1188
Waynesboro, Virginia 22980
Phone (703) 949-8311
Staunton (703) 886-6044

FALL FOLIAGE FESTIVAL — This is an annual event that comes during the final weeks of September and early weeks of October. Generally speaking a series of unconnected events take place on succeeding weekends consisting of cultural, art, athletic, hobby and varying interests. Additional events are added each year. The art show attracts some 300 artists and brings with it many visitors to the community.

History
Dating back to approximately 1764 and operating under the name of Teesville, we have today's Waynesboro. It has come about as the result of subsequent mergers between Basic City and Waynesboro among other evolutionary changes. General "Mad Anthony" Wayne, a very popular Revolutionary War hero, gave his name to the present city. History does not show the famed general coming to this locale. Heroes however, have a way of giving their names to people and places and so it is with Waynesboro.

Sports
The Waynesboro Country Club and Swannanoa Golf Course provide a challenge in this activity. Municipal tennis courts are well maintained and are situated in two separate sections of the community. Municipal swimming pools provide a cooling touch during the summer months. During the months of June and July the Waynes-

boro Generals, baseball entry into the Valley Baseball League, furnishes some top flight semi pro action. This is a league made up of college players. The major leagues, today, include a number of Waynesboro Generals of recent years.

Educational Institutions
FISHBURNE MILITARY SCHOOL, an historic military prep school for young men, is located in the heart of the downtown section. This respected institution boasts students from the United States and from most parts of the world.

Commonwealth of Virginia
The State of Virginia operates a school for employees of the state prison system. There is also an area law enforcement academy serving the region.

Geography
Waynesboro is situated in and between the west slope of the Blue Ridge Mountains and the Allegheny Mountains. It is approximately 140 miles from Washington, D.C., approximatley 90 miles from Richmond and about the same distance from Roanoke. I-64 connects the city to distant east-west points. This interstate is about nine miles from north-south I-81 and it is at this point that the two highways merge.

Air
Waynesboro is served by a small adequate airport for its chartered aircraft needs. Scheduled air service is provided from the Shenandoah Valley Airport some 15 miles away in Weyers Cave, Va. This airport serves Waynesboro, Staunton, and Harrisonburg. Service is provided by Henson Airlines, which has recently been purchased by Piedmont Airlines. This service provides connecting air service to various Piedmont hub points in such cities as Baltimore, Washington, and Charlotte. Some 25 miles away is the Charlottesville Airport which is also served by Piedmont Airlines. This is supplemented by commuter service.

Railroad and Bus
Amtrak offers nearby service as does Trailways.

Population and Political Entity
Population for this city runs about 15,500. This is an independent city and is contiguous to Augusta County and Nelson County. The City of Waynesboro and Augusta County are currently involved in annexation proceedings. It is conceivable that the city could ultimately enlarge in both area and population as the result of these proceedings.

Climate

The city enjoys four seasons and the temperature can be considered routinely moderate. During the winter there are periods of snow and during the summer there are days in the 90's.

— Virginia State Travel Service
Dogwood Blossoms Beautify the Countryside Near Roanoke

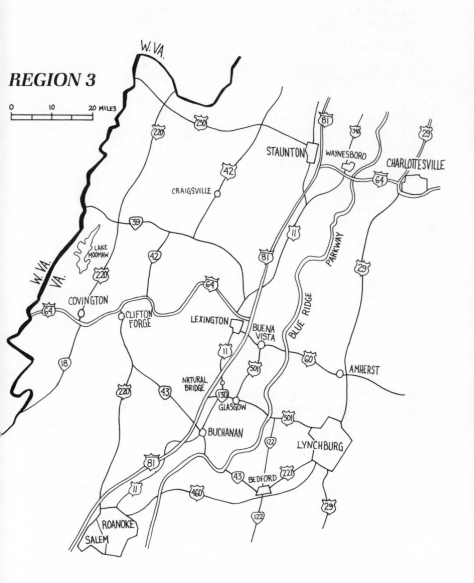

REGION 3

0   10   20 MILES

ALLEGHANY HIGHLANDS

Lodgings: (703)
Holiday Inn Covington, US 60 & 220, 962-4951
Town House Motel, W. Main St., Covington, 962-1161

Potpourri

This region, reminiscent of parts of Switzerland, is often called the Virginia Highlands. It is situated midway along the western border of the state.

Population here is about 28,000 persons. The breakdown shows Clifton Forge with about 5,000; Covington with some 9,000. Alleghany County's share comes to the remaining 14,000. This area is some 50 miles north of Roanoke. It is served by the C & O Railroad. Vehicular traffic is adequately served through US 220, US 60, and I-64. The latter ties in with I-81, so very important for north-south traffic.

Commercial air service can be secured at Roanoke or Weyers Cave. There is also some service available at Hot Springs or Lewisburg, W. Va. Private aircraft can be accommodated at a small airport located between Covington and Hot Springs.

The entire area is in the throes of annexation or consolidation proceedings. There is a school of thought advocating a consolidation of all three political sub-divisions. All of this should be resolved during the next few years.

COVINGTON

The earliest recorded settlement in Alleghany County took place in 1746. The early settlers were of Scotch-Irish ancestry. A small village known as Merry's Store was the original site for Covington. It was designated as a town in 1819 and was named for Peter Covington, the oldest resident at the time.

Covington is at the center of some of the best hunting and fishing in the east. Hunters report ample deer, bear, and turkey, while fishermen find the streams filled with trout and small-mouth bass.

ALLEGHANY CENTRAL RAILROAD — Located at the village of Intervale which is 2½ miles north of Covington on US 220. Now, here is an opportunity that you may never have had in your lifetime. Ride a real train, the steam engine kind with the old fashioned cars that bring one back to the way railroading was back in the 30's. You can take a two hour trip for a very reasonable passage price. Combine a picnic. For further information: Alleghany Central Corp., Rt. 5, P.O. Box 132, Covington, VA 24426, 703/962-2253.

THE HOMESTEAD — Resort; Hot Springs, VA 24445, 703/839-5500

CLIFTON FORGE

Potpourri

This city of approximately 5000 is in the northern part of the county. It is the home of the Dabney S. Lancaster Community College. Enrollment is about 1200.

The George Washington National Forest extends over much of the county. Lying along the Jackson River in both Alleghany and Bath Counties are some excellent hunting and fishing opportunities.

DOUTHAT STATE PARK — It lies on the Bath-Alleghany line just a few miles north of Clifton Forge.

GREEN PASTURES — 18-acre recreation area with swimming, picnicking, and camping. There is also an interesting picnic area at Humpback Bridge which is located three miles west of Covington. The Bridge was built in 1835 and was in use until 1929. Now, it is preserved as a wayside park.

LAKE MOOMAW at the Gathright Dam on the Jackson River is a good bet for fishermen.

ALLEGHANY COUNTY

Potpourri

The economy of the area has been closely tied in to the rich natural resources to be found here. Water, forests, and minerals have been the backbone. Four-fifths of the 450 square miles of this area is in commercial forest land with hardwood species predominating. The supply of pulpwood supports the area's largest industrial plant. It is refreshing to note that the U. S. Forest Service inventory reports the annual growth of timber in excess of 3½ times the amount cut.

The land is mountainous with deep valleys, tantalizing rivers, and streams that flow past your camera's eye. Elevation varies from 1000 feet at Covington and Clifton Forge to about 4000 feet at the highest peaks.

The climate here is in keeping with the surrounding area. However, the average temperature in summer will be somewhat lower than in the area to the east. Snowfall will be somewhat heavier; though, not as severe as one might think.

THE ALLEGHANY FURNACES — This will carrry you back to the period between 1830 to 1925 when iron ore mining and smelting was a major industry here. It was here that cannons and cannon balls were manufactured for the Confederate Army.

FALLING SPRINGS FALLS — This waterfall cascades 200 feet into a gorge along US 220 ten miles north of Covington.

FORT YOUNG — Originally built by George Washington during the French and Indian Wars in 1756. By 1854 it had all disappeared. It was reconstructed according to Washington's plans. It may be seen near Exit 4 on I-64.

BEDFORD

Lodgings: (703)
Best Western Terrace House Inn, US 460W, 586-8286
Peaks of Otter Lodge & Restaurant, Blue Ridge Pkwy., 586-1081
Sportsmen's Inn Motel & Restaurant, Huddleston, 297-7532

Dining
Allegro, 1504 Longwood Ave., 586-2021
Bedford Restaurant, US 460W, 586-9874
Buddy's Family Restaurant, Blue Ridge Ave., 586-1670
Byrd's Restaurant & Svc. Stat, Moneta, 297-5142
The Cove, Moneta, 297-5461
Fisher's Restaurant, 503 4th St., 586-2233
Friar Tuck's, 117 N. Bridge, 586-9374
Genesis Restaurant, Goode, 586-1876
Goode's Country Kitchen, Rte. 1, 586-5278
Hardee's, Main St., 586-2682
Kentucky Fried Chicken, E. Main St., 586-3377
Kountry Korners, Thaxton, 586-2365
Lunch Box, 109 S. Bridge, 586-8460
Millstone Steak House, Rte, 5, 586-9291
Our Place, Huddleston, 297-7325
Pappy's Pizza, 1508 Longwood Ave., 586-8889
Peaks of Otter Lodge & Restaurant, Blue Ridge Pkwy., 586-1081
Pizza Hut, 870 E. Main, 586-8243
Rainbow Drive-In, 1504 Longwood Ave., 586-1111
Snak Shop, 104 N. Bridge, 586-0461
Sportsmen Inn, Huddleston, 297-7532
Sub Shop, 247 Depot St., 586-4281
Terrace House Restaurant, US 460W, 586-9442
Westbounder Restaurant, US 460E, 586-9054
Western Shop Restaurant, Thaxton, 586-5375

Potpourri
At the outset it is well to remember that Bedford County and Bedford City are two separate political entities. The city's population is about 6000 while the county is about 35,000. The community is some 25 miles from Lynchburg and about 35 miles from Roanoke. Principal highways serving the community are US 460 and US 221 as well as Va. 43.

There are two small airports in the immediate area. Commercial air service is available from both Lynchburg and Roanoke. Railroads serving the area are the Norfolk & Southern, Chessie, and Amtrak. Both Greyhound and Trialways supply the bus needs.

Elevation ranges from 900 feet to 4200 feet in the north. The community enjoys four seasons and averages 45" rainfall and 17" snowfall during the year.

Points of Note
This very scenic part of the state was first settled around 1700. It is the highest part of the Piedmont Plateau. The official beginning came in 1754 when the locale was named in honor of John Russell, Duke of Bedford.

ELKS NATIONAL HOME — This stately facility is located in Bedford. Each year the display of Christmas decorations captures the attention of viewers from many miles around.

BEDFORD MUSEUM — Interesting displays on the Civil War years.

POPLAR FOREST — Summer retreat for Thomas Jefferson is located in the county. It is reputed to be the first octagonal residence built in the country.

HOLY LAND U.S.A. — This 400 acre replica of the Holy Land in Israel is open to the public the year round. There are no admission charges but contributions are accepted. It is located on Va. 746 five miles from town. For additional information call: 586-2823.

PEAKS OF OTTER — Named after the hills of Scotland in 1700 by Charles and Robert Ewing they rise to 4001 feet. Located on the Blue Ridge Parkway with scenery that is incomparable. Visitors will find a lodge here with dining and lodging facilities, overlooking a lake.

Long John Silver's, US 60 E, 463-6086
The Side Porch, Buena Vista, 261-7771
Wattslynne Restaurant, Natural Bridge, 291-2673
Westmoreland Colony Buffet, Natural Bridge, 291-2364

Potpourri
The county seat of Rockbridge County has a population of 3500
people, more or less. Elevation here is 1152 feet. The leading industry here has to be education, for there are two colleges with an
enrollment that totals 3000.Incidentally, each school is responsible
for about 50% of the total. It's a beautiful historic town some three
miles away from I-81 and I-64. US 60 as well as US 11 supplies the
principal arterials for the community.

Lexington is a refuge from the pressure cooker society that so many
of us live in. It is more than a sleepy southern town. It is an extension
of 19th Century America cloaked in a strong traditional academic
vestment. Its beauty, grace, courtesy, and pride wrapped into a
package of gentility. It is going back into time when people had time
to ask about neighbors. It is a community that not only lives in the
past but proudly looks forward to a future of well educated, well
mannered individuals. It is a community surrounded by the most
beautiful scenery to be found any place. Neither town nor county
bulge at the seams with overpopulation. It is a region that is content

with its size. It appreciates the bounty that it derives from both countryside and heritage.

Take the time while you are here to enjoy the local spirit. Spend an extra day to relax, as you turn back the calendar to a Lexington of yesteryear.

VISITOR CENTER — It all begins at the Sloan House located at 107 East Washington Street, 703/463-3777. Martha Doss is the Director of the Department of Tourism. This is where you go for detailed information and assistance.

Do not be lulled, by our earlier description of the community, into thinking that you will be dealing with some sleepy headed souls. Far be it from that. We find that Ms. Doss and her people are just about the most professional people that we have encountered in our almost three decades in tourism. They have done their homework well. They know their community past and present. They can help you plan a thoroughly organized and fruitful stay. Don't pass up the opportunity.

WASHINGTON & LEE UNIVERSITY — Founded in 1749, it is the nation's sixth oldest college. It's a four year male liberal arts college with a coed law school. The school came upon hard times. Through the generosity of George Washington, in endowing 100 shares of James River Company stock in 1796, the school managed to survive.

It was in 1865, following the war, that Robert E. Lee became the college president. The Lee House was designed in 1869 to be the President's home. It is next door to the Lee-Jackson House which was built in 1843.

THE NEOCLASSICAL FRONT CAMPUS was designated as a National Historic Landmark in 1961. It was then that the Department of the Interior characterized Washington & Lee University as "one of the most dignified and beautiful campuses in the nation."

LEE CHAPEL & MUSEUM — This National Historic Landmark was built on the campus of W & L in 1867. It serves as a burial place for the General and his family. Lee's office is pretty much as it was when he last used it in 1870. The famed horse, Traveller, is buried in a plot outside the General's office. The Lee's museum contains items belonging to the Lee family. Among the portraits is the famous Peale portrait of George Washington. It is open to the public.

THE STONEWALL JACKSON HOUSE — It has been restored as a documentary historic site. Jackson was a professor at Virginia Military Institute and lived in Lexington from 1851 to 1861. Visitors will learn more about this famed soldier and at the same time learn

Virginia Military Institute Cadets on Parade, Lexington

about the town of Lexington during the time of Jackson. The gift shop has some very unique offerings for people interested in the era.

VIRGINIA MILITARY INSTITUTE — Founded in 1839, it is the oldest state supported military college in the nation. Its current mission is to continue to provide an undergraduate education program of the highest quality in a military environment.

On May 15, 1864, the Corps of Cadets engaged as a unit in battle at New Market. They were credited with helping to turn the tide in favor of the Confederate forces there. Numbered among some of the prominent names associated with VMI are Stonewall Jackson, a professor there for 10 years. Then, there was Matthew Fontaine Maury, the "Pathfinder of the Seas," who taught physics and astronomy from 1868 until 1872. Graduating in 1901 was George C. Marshall, famed army Chief of Staff during World War II, author of The Marshall Plan, and Secretary of State.

The cadet barracks have also been designated as a National Historic Landmark.

Full dress parades are held on the parade grounds, weather permitting, on Fridays during fall and spring at 4:15 PM. Formal guard mount is a daily occurrence, weather permitting, each day at 12:30 PM.

VIRGINIA MILITARY INSTITUTE MUSEUM — This houses the Cadet Chapel and has a large oil painting depicting the Cadet charge at the Battle of New Market. Flags of the 26 states in the Union when the school was founded are around the balcony. Exhibits representing the history and tradition of the Institute are housed here. They include the coat Jackson used while teaching, the bullet that pierced his raincoat at the Battle of Chancellorsville as well as exhibits interpreting cadet life at VMI past and present. There is even a replica display of a cadet room in the Barracks, open to the public.

GEORGE C. MARSHALL MUSEUM AND LIBRARY — The museum traces the career of this distinguished American with particular emphasis on the eras of the two World Wars and the Marshall Plan. On display is the Nobel Peace Prize that was awarded to General Marshall in 1953. Also on display is the Academy Award Oscar presented to General Frank McCarthy, also an alumnus, as producer of the movie "Patton." Open to the public.

STONEWALL JACKSON MEMORIAL CEMETERY — This is located on the southern edge of town and dates back to 1797. Buried here are General Jackson, hundreds of Confederate veterans and two former governors. The Valentine statue done in 1891 faces the south. Open to the public.

SPECTATOR SPORTS — Intercollegiate schedules are maintained by both schools and further particulars can be secured from the respective athletic departments.

Cultural Attractions
ROCKBRIDGE CONCERT-THEATER SERIES and FINE ARTS WORKSHOP.

SCENIC DRIVE EXTRAORDINAIRE — Take Va. 39 from Lexington and drive west through the Goshen Pass, if you want to preview what Paradise must be like. You will drive along the banks of the Maury River and be treated to nature at its primeval best. Bring a picnic basket and your bathing wear. But, whatever you do, don't forget your camera.

WATER PEOPLE — There are numerous creeks and rivers in the area that those of you actively inclined might be interested in traversing. You might want to contact James River Basin Canoe Livery Ltd., Rt. 4, Box 109-A, Lexington, VA 24450, 261-7334.

HISTORIC GARDEN WEEK — This is always a big event here. Contact the Visitor Center for further information.

ALONG THE CHESSIE NATURE TRAIL — This is a yellow folder that you should be able to get from the Visitor Center. It is

labeled as "A guide to the footpath between Lexington and Buena Vista, Virginia." We think that you would find this to be most useful.

SUMMER THEATER — Henry Street Playhouse & Stock Company runs at the old Troubador Theatre in the town's historic district. During the months of June, July, and August you will be able to be thoroughly entertained by a troupe that shares in the proceeds of the box office. True to the tradition of early American theater, all actors and crew are issued shares of stock.

NATURAL BRIDGE — If you take I-81 south or US 11 south, the distance is about 12 miles to Natural Bridge. The natural stone bridge is one of the Seven Natural Wonders of the World. It was originally granted by King George III to Thomas Jefferson and surveyed by George Washington. The bridge is open daily as are the recently discovered caverns. The spectacular "Drama of Creation" is a lights and music show presented at night. Further information: 291-2121. Additional attractions that you might consider while you are at the "Bridge" are the Natural Bridge Zoo, Wax Museum, and Monster Museum.

Climate
The weather is comparable to that of the surrounding area. There are four seasons with some hot days and some cold days and a modicum of snow during the winter.

Transportation
Commercial air service from Roanoke, which is about 45 miles away. Greyhound operates the buses. Both I-81 and US 11 are excellent highways coming in and out of the area.

LYNCHBURG

Lodgings: (804)
Ash's Brick Tourist Cottages, 2125 Lakeside Dr., 239-5434
Crist Motel, 2815 Candlers Mountain Rd., 237-2986
Forest Hills Motel, 2032 Lakeside Dr., 239-4435
Harvey's Motel, Wards Rd., 239-2611
Lynchburg Motor Court, 2108 Lakeside Dr., 239-1742
Days Inn Motel, Candlers Mountain Rd., 847-8655
Econo Travel Motor Hotel, Rt. 29S, 847-1045
Lynchburg Hilton Hotel, 2900 Candlers Mountain Rd., 237-6333
Holiday Inn, Rt. 29S, 847-4424
Ramada Inn, 1500 E. Main St., 845-5975
Sheraton Inn, Rt. 29, Odd Fellows Rd., 847-9041

Restaurants: (804)
Fast Food
Arby's, 2500 Memorial Ave, 846-7596
  2110 Wards Road, 237-4202
Burger King, 2104 Wards Rd., 237-3584
  2424 Memorial Ave., 847-5250
Church's Fried Chicken, 1201 Campbell Ave., 845-5322
Dairy Queen, 3033 Old Forest Rd., 384-8801
  4915 Fort Ave., 239-2004
Hardee's, 1125 Main St., 847-0192
  Wards Road, 237-3839
Long John Silver's Seafood Shoppe, Wards Rd., 239-1316
  2505 Memorial Ave., 239-5380
  8101 Timberlake Road, 239-2004
McDonald's, 2135 Wards Rd., 239-7852
  3108 Old Forest Road, 384-8003
Waffle House, 5224 Fort Ave., 239-1204
Wendy's Old Fashioned Hamburgers, 7909 Timberlake Rd., 237-4543
  2117 Wards Road, 237-0029
  2510 Memorial Avenue, 528-1383
Yellow Submarine, 3313 Old Forest Rd., 384-7294

Family/Cafeteria
Ashley's Southern Fried Chicken, 2225 Langhorne Rd., 847-0000
Barbara's Country Cookin', 2034 Lakeside Dr., 237-6279
Bonanza Sirloin Pit, 2420 Wards Rd., 239-8756
Family Fish House, 3220 Old Forest Rd., 284-5913
Golden Corral Steak House, 6201 Fort Ave., 237-5189
The Ground Round, 2819 Candlers Mountain Rd., 237-1692
Howard Johnson's Restaurant, 2004 Wards Rd., 239-5315
Morrison's Cafeteria, River Ridge Mall, 237-6549
PJ's, 545 Oakley Ave., 847-7990

Samuel's Cafeteria, The Plaza, 846-0466
Western Sizzlin' Steak House, 2160 Wards Rd., 239-2632
C & S Cafe, 1905 Old Forest Rd., 847-8221

Chinese
Empire Garden Restaurant, 2124 Wards Rd., 239-1717
King's Island Restaurant, 2804 Old Forest Rd., 384-0066

Italian
Chris & Sal's, 917 Main St., 528-3789
Giovanni's Pizza & Subs, River Ridge Mall, 239-3737
Monte Carlo Restaurant, 3230 Old Forest Rd., 384-9300
Pizza Hut, 4901 Fort Ave., 239-9557
  2309 Bedford Ave., 846-5348
  3025 Old Forest Rd., 384-0079
  2413 Memorial Ave., 845-1433
Pizza Inn, 5006 Boonsboro Rd., 384-1941
  6010 Fort Ave., 239-6211
  2605 Memorial Ave., 847-1031
Sal's Italian Restaurant, Fort Hill Village, 237-6256

Continental
Aberdeen Barn, 4000 Murray Pl., 847-9085
Cruikshanks Publick House, Langhorne Rd. Shopping Center, 845-5240
Emil's Le Chalet, Boonsboro Shopping Center, 384-2861
Landmark Steak House & Lounge, 6113 Fort Ave., 237-1884
Sachiko Continental Restaurant, 126 Old Graves Mill Rd., 237-5655
The Eagle Restaurant & Lounge, 1030 Main St., 846-3898
Johnny Bull's Restaurant & Imbibery, 2900 Candlers Mountain Rd., 237-6333
The Red Lobster, River Ridge Mall
Steak & Ale Restaurant, 7118 Timberlake Rd., 239-5450
Crown Sterling, 6120 Fort Ave., 239-7744
Charley's, River Ridge Mall, 237-5988

That Seafood Place, Rt. 29S, 845-0011
Top of the James Restaurant & Lounge, 1500 E. Main St., 845-5975
Cedar Street, 3009 Old Forest Rd., 284-7118
Holiday Inn South, Rt. 29S, 847-4424
Sow's Ear, 1 Wadsworth St., 528-2620
Sword & Kilt Restaurant, River Ridge Mall, 239-5611
T. C. Trotter's, 2496 Rivermont Ave., 528-0665
G. T. Brooks, 40001 Murray Pl., 845-7427

Dinner Theatre
Historic Joseph Nichols Tavern Dinner Theatre, 5th & Madison,
528-3305

Lynchburg
This city of approximately 70,000 persons got its name from John
Lynch who built a ferry across the James River in 1757. It is believed
that in 1791 Lynch built the first tobacco warehouse in the country
here.

This is an industrially oriented community and serves as a shopping
center for the central part of the state. It is a progressive community
undergoing constant change.

Though manufacturing is important to the economy, of equal
importance is education. Among the schools of higher learning are
Lynchburg College, Randolph Macon Women's College, Liberty
Baptist College, and Central Virginia Community College. Some 12
miles from the city is Sweet Briar College, a very well known private
women's college.

Lynchburg has a very proud cultural heritage. Much of it is centered
at its very well equipped Fine Arts Center where art, dance, drama,
and music take place. Lynchburg residents have ample opportunity
to actively develop their talents as active participants of those
aforementioned disciplines. There is also a place for those that
appreciate without the benefit of the doing. We would refer to the
modern auditorium that seats approximately 550 people for theater,
symphony concerts, pops, jazz, or ballet.

In addition to this there are performances at the restored Western
Hotel, in the downtown area, by a local theatrical company. There is
a series of dinner theater performances.

Geography
The city is located in Central Virginia and enjoys four regular
seasons with some extremely warm days during the summer. The
winter will have its share of cold days and will receive some 3-4
snows during the season. The city is built on hills resulting in varying
elevation from 500 feet to 1300 feet.

This city is a hub for a number of major highways. US 501, US 460 as well as US 29 intersect. I-81 will run parallel to US 29. The city enjoys a strategic location within the state having easy access to Roanoke, Charlottesville, and Richmond.

The local airport serves the community through Piedmont Airlines and Air Virginia. Rail service is furnished by Amtrak, Chessie, and Norfolk & Southern. Greyhound and Trailways share the bus honors.

Spectator Sports
There are many devotees of high school athletics in the area. At the college level there is an ample schedule of intercollegiate events offered by the local institutions in a full range of sports. This is supplemented by nearby schools such as the University of Virginia, VMI, and Roanoke College. There is a local entrant in the Class A Carolina League — The Lynchburg Mets offering baseball fans an opportunity to view the stars of tomorrow.

Participant Sports
Tennis and golf abound in the area. Waterfront activities like fishing, hunting, swimming, and boating are close at hand. Nearby Smith Mountain Lake offers 20,000 acres of water to satisfy the wants of visitors to this locale.

Sightseeing

Lynchburg is a city of many fine homes of contemporary design with well kept lawns. Driving through the residential section treats the eye to pleasing examples of modern day America. By the same token architectural buffs will find many homes that have been returned to the majesty and grandeur that endured in the 19th Century.

High above the James River reclines POINT OF HONOR, a home built by Patrick Henry's physician, Dr. George Cabell, Sr. The striking mansion is built in Federal residential style. The building is open to the public Tuesdays through Saturdays from 1:00 PM to 4:00 PM all during the year excepting January and February. Further information may be obtained from the Lynchburg Museum System, P.O. Box 60, Lynchburg, VA 24505; 800/847-1459.

Historic residential areas of the 19th Century can be seen on Court House Hill, Garland Hill, Daniel's Hill, Diamond Hill, and Rivermont Avenue. Located in Riverside Park is the Miller-Claytor House, one of the city's oldest buildings. It is open to the public.

Make certain that you visit the Old Courthouse which is an example of Greek Revival. The courtroom has been restored to its earlier appearance. On exhibit are items dating back to Lynchburg's early history. Monument Terrace is a memorial staircase rising to the Old Courthouse from Church Street that justifies your viewing. The building is restored to its 1855 appearance and is the home of the Lynchburg Museum. The building is located at 901 Court Street. For further information: 804/847-1459.

It is at 1313 Pierce Street that stands the home of Anne Spencer a noted poet of great international repute. Her working studio, "EdanKraal" is directly behind the home of this celebrated participant of the Harlem Renaissance.

Out Of Town Sightseeing

BEDFORD — You might enjoy visiting the Bedford Museum which has interesting displays on the Civil War years. In Bedford County is Poplar Forest, the summer retreat that Thomas Jefferson

designed in 1806. It is supposed to be the first octagonal residence built in this country.

HOLY LAND U.S.A. — Located five miles from Bedford is a 400 acre replica of the Holy Land in Israel. It is open the year round. There is no admission charge; however, contributions are accepted. Located in Va. 746 five miles from Bedford. Further details may be secured by calling: 703/586-2823.

APPOMATTOX — On Va. 24 two miles north of town is the Appomattox Court House National Historical Park. This is a restored historic village of some 27 structures where General Lee surrendered to General Grant marking an end to the Civil War. Open to the public with a nominal admission fee. Further information: 804/352-8987.

HISTORIC APPOMATTOX STATION ARTS & CRAFTS CENTER, INC. — Handicrafts including dolls, knitting, quilts and other items done by county residents.

ACTIVE VACATION SUGGESTIONS

Virginia's "highway in the sky," the Skyline Drive is your avenue to escape from that regimented 20th Century civilization. Here, traffic can not exceed a safe and sound 35 miles per hour as it traverses the Shenandoah National Park along the peaks of the Blue Ridge Mountains.

There is no need to belabor the fact that the foliage here at the Fall of year would cause tingles to overpower a convention of landscape painters. The other seasons have equal compensations as one views the scenery from any of 71 roadside overlooks. If you want to see more than forest flowers, vines, and trickling streams you may opt for the plentiful wildlife. Maybe you will chance some chipmunks, squirrels, white-tailed deer — maybe a black bear or even a bobcat. Then, for the bird watcher, there are more than 200 species that share the park with the other animals.

Naturalist programs and hikes are scheduled by the rangers at the various visitor centers. Hikers are able to choose from more than 400 miles of trails, including a fairly smooth 90 mile stretch of the famous Maine to Georgia Appalachian Trail. There are trails leading to waterfalls, the largest being the breathtaking 93 foot cascade called Overall Run Falls. The unpaved dirt roads that are used for administrative purposes are also open to hikers and joggers with the added assurance that there will be no bicycle or private vehicular traffic upon them.

The biker is not forgotten. Front Royal, at the northern tip of Shenandoah National Park, is part of a loop trail developed by a non-profit bicycling organization, Bikecentennial. The trail's course starts in Washington, runs west to Front Royal, south to Harrisonburg and Waynesboro, east to Richmond, and north through Fredericksburg back to the nation's capital.

Horseback riders have more than 150 miles of horse trails and administrative roads. Incidentally, horses and ponies can be rented for guided trail rides April through early November at Skyland and at Big Meadows from late May through October.

The Shenandoah River offers an opportunity for the canoeists. This is dramatic scenery. The river's wider south fork is particularly popular. There are several firms that can assist you with the boating equipment such as: Shenandoah River Outfitters of Luray, 340 Outfitters of Front Royal, Downriver Canoe Company of Bentonville and James River Runners of Scottsville also supply gear, guides and whatever. This latter company also offers inner-tube trips on the James River, near the historic pole-ferry at Hatton. Canoeists can join the annual Virginia Championship Canoe Races held the last weekend in April each year on the Shenandoah at Front Royal.

In the steep streams in the park's lower boundaries, fishermen can daily catch and remove up to five Eastern Brook Trout that are a minimum of eight inches long. The Staunton and Rapidan Rivers are managed as fish-for-fun streams, where all catches must be returned to the water alive.

Now for those of you with a flare for the bit more adventurous, there is a spectacular aerial view of the Blue Ridge Mountains and the valley below. Visitors with hang gliders can use the breezes at Hogback Ridge, Dickey Hill and Miller's Head. You'll need your own equipment and proof of a Hang-3 rating to obtain a permit from a ranger at any of the park's entrance stations. We don't have the word on the Ultra-Lights so owners of that type equipment should inquire in advance with park authorities.

Campsites are also available for those that long for that extra bit of nature at first hand. There are five campgrounds with fire grates and the necessary comfort stations. Naturally, there are some camp stores to keep you up with the vital necessities. For the real adventurer, there is the back country where you can pitch your tent. Open fires are restricted but there are trailside shelters offering fireplaces. Back country camping permits are available free at the park entrance stations and at campgrounds as well as visitor centers.

Park wildlife is offered sanctuary from the hunter.

Additional information can be secured from the Virginia Division of Tourism in Richmond.

SKI BUFFS

One does not think of this state as the ski capital of the world nor of even eastern USA. But it is well to remember that there are redeeming features in skiing here. During the winter season, you do not have the bitter cold that one often finds in New England.

WINTERGREEN — A year-round resort 43 miles southwest of Charlottesville. Three new expert slopes with a 1003 foot vertical drop, a new triple chairlift and a new warming hut enhance the ski season here. The resort has an excellent snowmaking system for its 83 acres of slopes. Their snowmaking equipment is reputed to be the world's most sophisticated.

Located off US 29 — main complex 3500'; vertical slope 1003'; ski school.

BRYCE RESORT (BAYSE) — Located in the historic Shenandoah Valley, Bryce Mountain is another year-round retreat offering winter fun as well as grass skiing in summer and fall. Two double chairlifts and three rope tows take skiers to the tops of four trails where the vertical drop is 500 feet.

Located at I-81 at Exit 69; base elevation 1250'; ski school.

CASCADE MOUNTAIN SKI RESORT — Located in southwest Virginia about 15 miles east of Galax, this relatively new resort has six trails designed especially for beginners and families.

Located off I-77 north of Fancy Gap; base elevation 3000'; ski school.

MASSANUTTEN VILLAGE — Near Harrisonburg and 125 miles southwest of the nation's capital. The resort features nine slopes and trails with a vertical drop of 795 feet, four chairlifts and a J-bar. Massanutten offers some of the state's steepest skiing along with a 5600 foot run.

Located I-81 at Exit 64; base elevation 1730'; ski school.

THE HOMESTEAD — A Virginia resort, steeped in tradition, is located at Hot Springs, 75 miles north of Roanoke. The gentle mountain is well suited to beginners and to advanced skiers who like to make long, carved turns in the snow. There are five slopes and three trails, a double chairlift, T-bar, and rope tow.

Cross Country skiers can appreciate a 105 mile stretch of the Blue Ridge Parkway, which closes to motor traffic during heavy snowfalls. Here skiers find unusually quite, peaceful surroundings and a spectacular view of the valleys below.

Located US 220; base elevation 2500'; 3 trails and 5 slopes; ski school.

MOUNT ROGERS NATIONAL RECREATION AREA — Excellent cross country skiing in high elevation areas reached by plowed roads. Additional information can be secured from the people at the park.

Bicycling

In the recent past, pro bicycle teams sped through winding stretches of Virginia's highways as they passed lush green farmland, picturesque towns with cobblestone streets and the rolling hills made famous as the result of historic battles. It seems as if the pros are now learning what amateur cyclists had known for years. Virginia is an ideal backdrop for the sport.

Mapped out by Bikecentennial, a national touring bicyclist organization, the Virginia Loop trail offers 568 miles of pedaling. It begins in Washington and snakes down through country roads through Front Royal, Charlottesville, Richmond, and Fredericksburg before returning to its starting point. The scenery along the way is exceptional. The route passes farms, fields, and fish hatcheries in the unequaled beauty of Virginia's western Shenandoah Valley. The cyclist might even discover the Memms Bottom covered bridge — the longest of nine covered bridges in the state.

For the avid biker who looks for the challenge, there is always the mile high Skyline Drive and the Blue Ridge Parkway. These routes combine demanding mountainous terrain with scenic wonder. The 319 miles of bikeway provide great possibilities for the dual enjoyment of biking with camping.

We would also remind the cyclist that the various State and National Park facilities within the area of western Virginia offers great cycling possibilities.

Blue Ridge Parkway

From atop the Blue Ridge Mountains Thomas Jefferson once described the view by saying, "This scene is well worth a voyage across the Atlantic." We should hasten to remind the reader that back in the Jeffersonian era one did not jet across the Atlantic. It was a long trip by sail. So if the sacrifice was worth it, we can certainly say that this same spectacular scenery awaits with an easier price tag. What we mean to say is that it is easy for those of us today to drink in the scene from the top of the Blue Ridge. The Blue Ridge Parkway is within a comfortable day's drive of eight eastern states.

Beginning at Afton Mountain, thirty miles west of Jefferson's home of Charlottesville and just a mile or so from Waynesboro is where it commences. It meanders southward through Virginia for 218 miles. No commercial traffic is allowed on the "skyland highway" and the safe and sane 45 miles per hour speed limit allows the sightseers the opportunity to take in the ever changing beauty of each section.

The pink dogwood and snowdrops give way to the purples and reds of the catawba rhododendron and flame azaleas, gently rolling plateaus with open meadows of yellow fieldcress give way to deepening green forests. All along the Parkway, vacationers can observe more species of flora than are found on the entire continent of Europe.

After a pleasant ascent through thick stands of tall pines and oaks, visitors suddenly find themselves back in the bright light of day and the road clinging to the side of a 3000 foot mountain. Below the valley floor resembles a giant patchwork quilt of brilliant yellows, greens, and golds.

Several exits from the Parkway can lead you to a variety of adventures. Reed's Gap exit heads east to Wintergreen where there is skiing, tennis, golf, swimming, horseback riding. You might care to dine at Rodes Farm Inn, a restored 19th Century farm house serving traditional Virginia country fare.

Over the Blue Ridge Mountains from Wintergreen is Sherando Lake with more than 100 campsites. Cyrus McCormick's farm and workshop where the reaper was invented. To the west is Douthat State Park featuring a 70 acre lake that is well stocked with rainbow trout.

On the parkway itself, there are numerous overlooks for enjoying the scenery as well as interpretive signs which speak of the points of interest as well as the recounting of historical facts. Visitor-use areas and information centers are scattered along the Parkway.

You pass Lexington, the Peaks of Otter, and the Washington National Forest. In Roanoke, we remind you of the largest collection of steam engines in the Transportation Museum and all of the other attractions of that city.

There are such scenic waysides as Smart View, Devil's Backbone, and the Saddle Line. This is the route to the Parkway's biggest attraction: Mabry Mill. More than a monument to the native ingenuity of the pioneers who settled the region, Mabry Mill is a working crafts center. The water powered grist mill is still in use and the sweet odors of hot apple butter and sorghum molasses lace the air throughout the year. Not to be forgotten is the sound of the blacksmith's hammer on the anvil.

After taking the self guided tour that illustrates a mint and whiskey still and the tools of the shoemaker, you can dine at Mabry Mill's Restaurant on buckwheat cakes made from flour ground fresh that morning. All of this can be accompanied by the picking and singing of local musicians performing the oldtime Appalachian tunes.

Now, for those of you that prefer getting off the beaten path you might drive the eastern face of the Blue Ridge for a visit to Fairy Stone State Park. This is the only place where nature has created tiny crosses of staurolite crystals — yours for the digging. Shot Tower Historical State Park is on the Parkway's western side, along with Big Walker Lookout and Dry Gulch Junction, a re-created old wild west town. In close proximity to those are Claytor, Hungry Mother, and Grayson Highlands state parks.

At the southernmost end of Virginia's Blue Ridge Parkway, visit Mrs. Orlen Puckett's cabin on Groundhog Mountain. A midwife who lived to be 102, Mrs. Puckett's home like other cabins scattered along the Parkway, chronicles the life and times of the pioneers who followed Daniel Boone on their westward march. Vacationers can watch at Groundhog authentic Appalachian crafts made at cottage industries. Nearby Groundhog Mountain Resort features chalets, a lodge and championship 18-hole golf.

The Blue Ridge Parkway is a peaceful and incomparably beautiful modern motorist trail that the 1980's pioneer can comfortably enjoy. It is a wonderful respite from the "Indianapolis 500" atmosphere that prevails on the Interstates that we so depend upon. Why not extend and enjoy your life by detouring from the stopwatch existence that so many of us live by. Try the Blue Ridge Parkway. It belongs to you and there isn't a single toll booth to skirt.

Golfing

The golfer doesn't have to forsake his game when he visits western Virginia. At Wintergreen resort nestled in the mountians is a par-71 course designed by Ellis Maples, past president of the golf architect trade association. Complement your game by viewing the 50 mile vista of the Blue Ridge Mountains and the Shenandoah Valley.

Sitting atop Afton Mountain in the Blue Ridge is Swannanoa Golf Course. Quoting one enthusiast, "it's possible to play bad golf and yet have a good time because the view is so fantastic."

The Blue Ridge Parkway, the 105 mile-long Skyline Drive and I-81 form major north-south by-ways from which visitors can meander down the backbone of the Blue Ridge. The 200 mile long Shenandoah Valley is a veritable gold mine of attractions. In New Market along with the battlefield is the Shenvalee Golf Club. It's a par 70 layout complete with three lakes, elevated greens.

Caverns County Club Resort, with 8000 yards of bentgrass greens along the banks of the Shenandoah River, is just a few miles from world-famous Luray Caverns. In nearby Harrisonburg, the Lakeview Golf Club has a 27 hole layout complete with four water holes. Massanutten Mountain Greens, located 10 miles east of Harrisonburg, features lateral water on four holes and water hazards on four others.

Hot Springs, located at the edge of the George Washington National Forest, offers Cascades Golf Club. It has been called one of the 30 greatest by Golf Digest. In addition, there is the Robert Trent Jones designed Lower Cascades Golf Club; and the Homestead, with its three 18-hole courses which have challenged golfers since 1893.

Visitors to Roanoke can take advantage of six courses. For that matter, we would point out that many of the private golf clubs will be pleased to give you privileges based on your own club membership. Discuss this with your pro before commencing your trip. Naturally, you can always talk golf with the people at the local chamber serving the community that you are passing through. Or better yet, why not call one of the golf clubs up when you hit their town.

Shenvalee Golf Course, located at new Market. The front nine are situated within the area of operations of the famed Battle of New Market.

Hit 'em straight and hit 'em true.

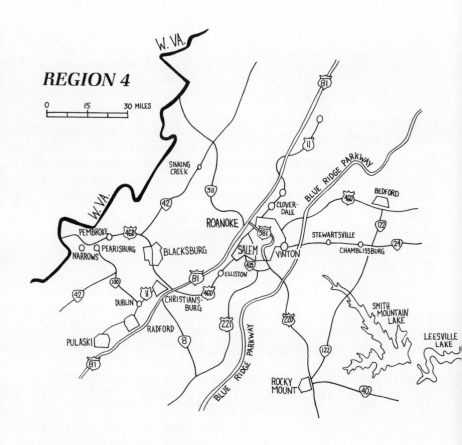

REGION 4

0   15   30 MILES

W. VA.

W. VA.

SINKING CREEK

42

311

ROANOKE

CLOVER-DALE

BLUE RIDGE PARKWAY

11

460

BEDFORD

PEMBROKE

460

581

STEWARTSVILLE

122

24

NARROWS

PEARISBURG

BLACKSBURG

SALEM

VINTON

CHAMBLISSBURG

415

100

11

81

ELLISTON

460

42

DUBLIN

CHRISTIANS-BURG

SMITH MOUNTAIN LAKE

LEESVILLE LAKE

RADFORD

220

PULASKI

8

221

81

122

BLUE RIDGE PARKWAY

ROCKY MOUNT

40

BLACKSBURG
Lodgings: (703)
Econo Lodge, 951-4242
Holiday Inn, 951-1330
Imperial Motor Lodge, 552-4011
Lake Terrace, 552-5131
Marriott Inn, 552-7001
Sheraton Red Lion Inn, 552-7770

Dining: (703)
Captain's Hidden Cove, 3000 Ramble Rd., 552-9509
Carol Lee Doughnuts, 133 College Ave., 552-6706
College Inn, 221 N. Main St., 552-9745
Country Kitchen, 1410 S. Main St., 552-5663
Cuckoo's Nest, 112 Turner St., 951-0001
Daddy's Money, 130 Jackson St., 552-6009
Domino's Pizza, 1315 S. Main St., 953-2643
Farmhouse Restaurant, Cambria St., 382-3965
Greek's Restaurant, 302 N. Main St., 552-8163
Harbor's Landing Fish Camp, 2606 Ramble Rd., 953-1548
Hardee's, 1311 S. Main St., 552-8843
Hokie House, 322 N. Main St., 552-0280
Holiday Inn, 3503 S. Main St., 951-1330
Little Caesar's Pizza, 871 Kabrich St., 951-4443
Longhorn Steak House, 708 N. Main St., 552-1350
Long John Silver's, 1202 S. Main St., 552-7188
McDonald's, 110 Price's Fork Rd., 552-2667
Marriott Inn, 900 Price's Fork Rd., 552-7001
Maxwell's, 1204 N. Main St., 552-9874
Mr. Fooz Sub Shop, 235 N. Main St., 552-4932
Philly Chee-Steak, 151 College Ave., 951-7747
Sheraton Red Lion Inn, 900 Plantation Rd., 552-7770
Wendy's, 701 N. Main St., 552-7139
Western Sizzlin' Steak House, 850 University City Blvd., 953-1660

CHRISTIANSBURG
Lodgings: (703)
Day's Inn, I-81, Exit 37 & US 11, 382-0261
Econo Lodge, I-81, Exit 37 & US 11, 382-6161

Dining
Bill's Restaurant, 1465 Roanoke St., 382-5372
Carlo Pizza Restaurant, 9 Radford St., 382-5366
Country Kitchen, 1085 Radford St., 382-9872
Famous Wiener Stand, 42 W. Main St., 382-3958

The FARMHOUSE
...more than just a restaurant

**SERVING THE AREA
FOR OVER TWENTY-ONE YEARS
CHRISTIANSBURG, VIRGINIA
382-4253**

Farmhouse, Cambria St., 382-4253
Hardee's, 103 Roanoke St., 382-6536
Long John Silver's, 1625 Roanoke St., 382-7024
McDonald's, Northgate Village; 382-3477
Smokehouse, 114 N. Franklin St., 382-2414
Stone's Cafeteria, Roanoke Road, 382-8970
Western Sizzler, 2380 Roanoke St., 382-1748

MONTGOMERY COUNTY

Population for this county is approximately 65,000; Christiansburg is approximately 10,600 while Blacksburg reports their population at 30,638. The area enjoys four seasons with a moderate climate for each season. Rainfall average runs about 41 inches per year with snowfall at about 20 inches per year. The area enjoys a very favorable humidity the year around. Elevations runs about 2100 feet. Distance from Roanoke to Christiansburg is 30 miles. It is 200 miles to Richmond. Distance between Blacksburg and Christiansburg is approximately 10 miles. Between Christiansburg and Radford it is about seven. Double that between Blacksburg and Radford.

Small aircraft can use the New River Valley Airport as well as the Virginia Tech Airport. Commercial air service is available at Woodrum Field in Roanoke. Rail service is furnished by the Norfolk & Southern while bus is offered by both Greyhound and Trailways. The motorist will find that US 460 will pass through the county and that I-81 and US 11 will pass through Christiansburg on its north-south course.

This county is blessed with incomparable education advantages in that two of the largest universities within the state are in the county and contiguous to the City of Radford. Virginia Tech with some 20,000 is located in Blacksburg. Radford University in Radford has approximately 12,000 students. New River Community College in nearby Dublin also serves the county's population.

The Montgomery Museum & Lewis Miller Regional Art Center will seriously address the needs of the community in offering a focus on the pre-historic and historic growth of southwestern Virginia. Further information on this new project can be secured by directing correspondence to them at: P.O. Box 418, Christiansburg, VA 24073.

Further information on Christiansburg and Montgomery County can be secured from: Christiansburg-Montgomery County Chamber of Commerce, P.O. Box 418, Christiansburg, VA 24073; 703/382-4251.

BLACKSBURG

Nestled between the Blue Ridge and the Allegheny Mountains is this college town with its many historic traditions. Originally, it was known as Draper's Meadow when it was settled as a small farming community in 1748. It was here that the Shawnees massacred most of the inhabitants. They did take a single captive, Mary Draper Ingles. Her story of escape and return is the basis for an annual outdoor theater pageant given in Radford during the summer months.

In the year 1798, the Black family contributed thirty-eight acres to the Draper Meadows community. It was at that time that William Black was granted by the General Assembly of Virginia a town charter. Thus, we have the name that the community today carries.

It was in the year 1872 that Dr. Henry Black petitioned the General Assembly to establish a land grant college in the community. That favorable cooperative action on the part of the state and the people of the community resulted in the start of Virginia Agricultural and Mechanical College and its first 43 students.

SMITHFIELD PLANTATION — This has been designated as an Official Virginia Historic Landmark. Smithfield was the birthplace of two Governors of Virginia. The home was first built in 1772. It is surrounded by the Virginia Tech campus. Visitors should turn from US 460 Bypass on Va. 314, taking the first left for two blocks thence take the next left — bear left and then turn right. We suggest that you secure a folder by the administrators of the Smithfield Plantation as it contains a helpful inset map along with particulars as to times that the facility is open to the public. Contact: Smithfield Plantation, Route 2, Blacksburg, VA 24060; 703/951-2060.

For general information on Blacksburg and the general area contact: The Greater Blacksburg Chamber of Commerce, 141 Jackson Street, Blacksburg, Virginia 24060; 703/552-4061.

VIRGINIA POLTECHNIC INSTITUTE AND STATE UNIVERSITY

It's a big mouthful to chew. This institution of higher learning has had many names since its official beginning on October 1, 1872. First it was known as Virginia Agricultural and Mechanical College. The General Assembly, effective March 4, 1896 changed it to Virginia Agricultural and Mechanical College and Polytechnic Institute. On June 23, 1944 the school's name was again changed to Virginia Polytechnic Institute. Effective June 26, 1970 it took on its present legal name, Virginia Polytechnic Institute and State University. It is known as VPI or Virginia Tech.

Its true ancestral beginning dates back to 1851 when a distinguished Methodist educator, Rev. Stephen Olin in conjunction with a leading area citizen, Col. William Ballard Preston opened the Olin & Preston Institute. Hard financial times came upon the school and it was compelled to close prior to the Civil War. Virginia Agricultural & Mechanical College based on authority granted by the Legislature reopened on October 1, 1872 with 43 students. Its student body was required to be members of the Corps of Cadets. In 1964, this requirement was dropped.

We can not resist quoting the book directly on this notable fact: "... the President's salary at $2,000 and professors' salaries at $1,500....

Charges to students not exempted by law were fixed at $30 for tuition and $10 for college fees; a cadet uniform cost $17.25. The cost of a session would be about $200." Virginia Tech today proudly numbers some 20,000 students of which 3,000 are graduate students. Approximately one third of the student body is composed of women. Today's Corps of Cadets accounts for approximately two percent of the total enrollment. Instruction is offered in seven academic colleges. Graduate work is offered in 65 fields of study. Doctoral programs cover 40 areas.

During the school year there is a full schedule of intercollegiate sports contests in a great variety of men's and women's events that can be viewed by the public from modern stadia facilities.

The community also enjoys a full spectrum of cultural events, many of which emanate from the campus of this institution. By way of illustration we have listed two of the many events held during the year: Brush Mountain Crafts Fair and the Annual Little International Livestock Show and Ham Sale.

Further information: Office of the Vice-President for Development and University Relations, Virginia Polytechnic Institute and State University, Blacksburg, VA 24061; VPISU: 703/961-6000.

BOTETOURT COUNTY

Lodgings: (703)
Traveltown Motel, Cloverdale, I-81, Exit 44, 992-1521
Howard Johnson's Motor Lodge, Troutville, I-81, Exit 44, 992-3000
Botetourt County
This county was formed from Augusta County in the year 1770 and was named after the Royal Governor of Virginia, Lord Botetourt. The county seat is Fincastle, which is listed on the National Register of Historic Places. The town is considered to be a notable example of a late 18th and early 19th Century town. Thomas Jefferson designed and furnished the plans for the county courthouse in 1818. It was here in the Town of Fincastle that William Clark of the famed Lewis & Clark expedition returned so that he could marry Judith Hancock.

The county is located in the southern entrance to the Shenandoah Valley lying in the valley between the Blue Ridge and the Alleghany Mountains. The county touches Roanoke County and is within 10 miles of the city and its airport. Passing through the county are US 220, US 11, and I-81. It is a natural lodging and dining spot as there are numerous facilities in the area. County population is about 24,000. Further information on the county can be secured from the Chamber of Commerce at Troutville, VA 24175, 703/992-1970.

GILES COUNTY

Nestled in a rather remote corner of the state is this very scenic and mountainous county. Though there is some industry within the boundaries of the County, many of its inhabitants commute to adjacent communities for their employment. US 460 traverses the length of the county on its way between Blacksburg and Princeton, W. Va. The advent of better highways has made Giles an easier destination for the outsider. Curves have been taken out of the steep and winding mountain highways. The challenge inherent to tortuous mountain roads no longer confronts the visitor to this area. Certain parts of the county will have an elevation in excess of 4000 feet.

The mountain scenery discloses that the land is stingy in its yield. Aside from the vegetable garden and the meat raised for family consumption there is little in the way of agriculture here. Today's better highways have resulted in a decided improvement in the local economy. Better highways have increased the flow of tourists through this beautiful mountain region. Conversely, it has given local residents easier access to employment beyond the barrier that was at one time created by the terrain.

Resort: (703)
Mountain Lake Hotel, Mountain Lake, VA 24136; 626-7121
Lodgings: (703)
Hapiday Motor Lodge, 401 N. Main St., Pearisburg; 921-1551

RADFORD

Lodgings: (703)
Claytor Lake Motel, I-81, Exit 33, Dublin, 674-4176
Day's Inn, I-81 & US 11, Christiansburg, 382-0261
Dogwood Lodge, US 11W, 639-9338
Econo Travel Motor Lodge, Roanoke Rd., Christiansburg,
382-6161
Executive Motel, S 11W, 639-1664
Tyler Inn & Tyler Motel, Hagy & Grove Streets, 639-3941
Holiday Inn, US 460S, Blacksburg, 951-1330
Ranch House Motel, Va. 100, Dublin, 674-4611
Red Carpet Inn, I-81, Exit 31, Pulaski, 980-2230

Dining
After Sundown Mexican Restaurant, Water & Main, Blacksburg,
951-9864
Angelo's Pizza, Main & Washington, Blacksburg, 951-2733
McPeak's Pub, Christianburg, 639-9915
Big Tee Family Restaurant, Roanoke Rd., Christiansburg, 382-2083
Bonanza, Gables Shopping Ctr., Blacksburg, 951-7365
Bonanza Sirloin Pit, US 11 & Va. 114, 639-6882
Buckner's Drive-In, Warren St., Christiansburg, 382-7557
Burger King, 204 Prices Fork Rd., Blacksburg, 951-8199
Chic 'N House Restaurant, Radford Rd., Christiansburg, 382-9872
Chris' Restaurant, Norwood St., Radford, 639-1997
Coffee Club, 221 Progress St., Blacksburg, 552-5213
College Inn, 221 N. Main, Blacksburg, 552-9745
Cuckoo's Nest, 112 Prices Fork Rd., Blacksburg, 951-0001
Daddy's Money, Jackson & Draper, Blacksburg, 552-6009
Dairy Queen, US 460S, Blacksburg, 552-5383
Dave's Hot Dogs, 216 N. Main, Blacksburg, 951-8172
Day's Inn Motel, I-81 & US 11, Christiansburg, 382-0261
Dog House Restaurant, First St., 639-9141
Dorothy's Drive-In, US 11, 639-6458
Downtowner Deli, 215 N. Main, Blacksburg, 951-0020
Fairlawn Drive-In Restaurant, Va. 114, 639-9184
The Farmhouse, Cambria St., Christiansburg, 382-3965
The Feed Box Drive-In, 1050 Radford Rd., Christiansburg,
382-0063
Frog Hollow Foods Bakery & Rest., 118 S. Main, Blacksburg,
951-9832
Golden Corral, US 11W, 639-2536
Granny's Old Fashioned Donuts, 1700 Norwood St., 639-5000
The Greek's Cellar & Rest., 302 N. Main, Blacksburg, 552-1876
Greek's Two, 211 Draper Rd., Blacksburg, 951-3728
Hank's Drive-In, US 11W, 731-1579
Harbor House, 3000 Ramble Rd., Blacksburg, 552-9509

Hardee's, 401 S. Main, Blacksburg, 552-8843
   103 Roanoke St., Christiansburg, 382-6536
Hardie House Restaurant, 1602 S. Main, Blacksburg, 552-1491
Hideout, 218 Tyler Ave., 639-0856
Hokie House Restaurant, 322 N. Main, Blacksburg, 552-0280
Holiday Inn Restaurant, US 460S, Blacksburg, 951-1330
The Inn Place, Tyler Hotel, Hagy & Grove, 639-2144
Jacob's Lantern Restaurant, 900 Prices Fork Rd., Blacksburg, 552-7001
Kentucky Fried Chicken, N. Franklin St., Christiansburg, 382-8957
   US 11W, Radford, 639-3231
Long John Silver's, US 11W, 731-1588
Our Hero, 1033 Norwood, 639-4634
Pizza Hut, 890 Kabrich St., Blacksburg, 552-4459
   310 Norwood St., 639-0800
Pizza Inn, N. Franklin St., Christiansburg, 382-4989
   US 11W, 639-9064
Ranch House Restaurant, US 100, Dublin, 674-4611
Roz-Lynn Steak House, Fair Akers, Dublin, 674-6471
Sheraton Red Lion Inn, 900 Plantation Rd., Blacksburg, 552-7770
Stone's Cafeteria, Roanoke Rd., Christiansburg, 382-8970
Tom Terrific's, Christiansburg, 639-9894
The Steak Place, US 460S, Blacksburg, 552-8441

Potpourri

Total population for the city is 14,000 which includes the total enrollment of approximately 6000 at Radford University. Contiguous to the city are the Counties of Montgomery and Pulaski. Its common sphere of interest appears to be closer to that of Montgomery County. For all intents and purposes there is a triangular concept for the communities of Radford, Blacksburg, and Christiansburg.

Radford is surrounded by beautiful rolling hills at an elevation of 1800 feet. Adjacent is the New River which is a major body of water in western Virginia. The city is located 41 miles west of Roanoke and eight miles from Christiansburg; 14 from Blacksburg and 17 from Pulaski. The city is connected north and south by I-81 and US 11. Travel to Blacksburg can be done easily by using Va. 114 which is locally referred to as the Powder Plant Road. Nearest commercial air service is available from Woodrum Field in Roanoke. Charter service is available at the New River Airport in nearby Dublin. Norfolk & Southern furnishes the rail service while Greyhound provides bus schedules.

The city enjoys the four seasons. By and large one would have to say that all of the seasons are moderate. Humidity is, for the most part, very pleasant. Rainfall will run about 40 inches per year and snow will run between 15-20 inches a winter.

There are a number of small sized industrial plants in the community as well as the Radford Army Ammunition Plant some eight miles from town. Radford University would have to be considered the largest employer within the city limits.

Radford University
The school was founded in 1910 as a State Normal School. Its principal mission was to prepare women for the teaching profession. In 1972 it became coeducational. In the year 1979, the institution was designated as a university. This beautiful campus is a mix of some of the older buildings tastefully blended with the very modern multi-story complexes. Enrollment is close to 6000 of which approximately one third are men. Enrolled in graduate work are some 800 students.

Undergraduate degrees are offered in 42 specific areas within the four schools: Arts and Sciences; Business and Professional; Education; and Fine Arts.

The University is currently involved in 11 intercollegiate sports. Schedules for the various teams may be secured from the athletic department.

Further information on the school can be secured by contacting: Radford University, Radford, VA 24142, 703/731-5371.

The Long Way Home
This is the only outdoor historical drama in the state. It will be entering its 14th season in 1984. Sponsored by the New River Historical Society, this drama depicts a story that took place in 1755. This tells the story of Mary Draper Ingles and her heroic adventure as she made her 850 mile escape through the wilderness to give warning of a forthcoming attack. We also get an insight into the feared Shawnee warriors that inhabited the area. The saga is re-enacted in the Ingles Homestead Amphitheater at her homesite and grave. The season generally commences on the third Friday in June and extends to Labor Day. The visitor can use I-81 and get off at Exit 34. It is west on Norwood Street (Route 232), principal street of the city. For further information contact: The Long Way Home, P.O. Box 711, Radford, VA 24141.

For further information on Radford you may contact: Radford City Chamber of Commerce, 103 Third Avenue, Radford, VA 24141, 703/639-2202.

ROANOKE AND MORE
By William J. Evitts

The Roanoke area is one of the best-kept secrets on the East Coast.

While three of every four Virginians live in the humid flats of Tidewater, Roanoke sits tucked in a gorgeous mountain bowl between the Blue Ridge and the Appalachians. It's a city of approximately 100,000, anchoring a metropolitan area of over 200,000. Roanoke's an urban center with easy charm, a classy city on the edge of the Blue Ridge Parkway. The ony drawback to the place is that it's so lovely, and there's so much to do, that on those Fall or Spring days when high pressure comes through and you can count the hemlock needles on Mill or Tinker Mountains, your heart breaks with the beauty of it all and it's a heroic effort just to do any work at all.

Roanoke is simply the only real city anywhere in the region. Its nearest urban competitor is Greensboro. In consequence, Roanoke is the retail, wholesale, financial, medical, cultural and governmental hub of an enormous area. In its metropolitan area are three private colleges (2 liberal arts — Roanoke and Hollins — and one business college) and a Community college. It is a brief drive away from many other public and private schools, including Radford, V.M.I., Washington & Lee, and Virginia Tech. It sits on the Interstate system and has excellent air connections. And it's still a secret known by few.

The physical beauty of the place hits you first. The charm of the people impresses you second. Then, slowly, it dawns on you that these rural virtues of nature and neighborliness support a very urbane community.

Consider: Roanoke has a Symphony, a Youth Symphony, 2 Civic Centers (one with both Coliseum and Auditorium), semiprofessional ballet, an Opera Society, a Chamber Music Society, and both amateur and professional theatre. One sure stop in the area is Center in the Square, which contains a Science Museum with planetarium, Mill Mountain Theatre, a historical museum, a regional arts council, and the Roanoke Museum of Fine Arts. Center is located on the old Market Square, where farmers sell from stalls as they have since the 1880's. That combination tells you a lot about Roanoke.

Roanoke is, as cities go, relatively new. Incorporated only in 1882, it was a creation of the Norfolk and Western (now Norfolk Southern) Railway. Until the 1910's Roanoke was a pretty rough place. Saloons outnumbered stores, and the town looked like a mushroom growth on top of the Valley salt marshes where animals used to gather. (It was the marshes that gave the Roanoke City area one of its early names — Big Lick). But in time the builders replaced the boomers, and Roanoke settled down. Only in its lack of pretension and its openness to new ideas, new people, and new ventures can you catch a glimpse of the old rough and ready railroad town.

As one result of its industrial past, Roanoke today has a fascinating Transportation Museum, in Wasena Park on Wiley Drive. Trains are the centerpiece, of course, and they have some classics. Occasionally the Norfolk Southern still runs steam excursions with the sleek, powerful J-611 engine up front. Roanoke's a mecca for train buffs.

The entire area has always been a crossroads. Look at a map. The Great, or Shenandoah, Valley runs like a funnel from south central Pennsylvania through Western Maryland, and it was down this chute that German and Scotch-Irish settlers came in the mid 18th century. The old town names show the non-English heritage: Dublin, Fincastle, Glasgow, Strasburg. Religious groups gave the region a lot of its character, and gave their communities names like Salem — now a thriving part of the Roanoke Valley. You can still see some of the Old Believers (as several sects are collectively referred to), plainly dressed, bonneted women and black-clad men, direct links to the Moravian and Mennonite communities that make the "Pennsylvania Dutch" country famous.

In Roanoke, the north-south Valley meets a gap in the Blue Ridge. Traffic — whether migrating herds, wandering Indians, settlers, railroaders, or twentieth century motorists — just naturally mixes here. The highways are often on top of the old Indian trails, like Route 460 to Lynchburg, or 220 South towards Carolina. Much of Route 11 in the north part of the Roanoke Vally overlays the Great Valley Road, 18th Century America's busiest thoroughfare.

The valley chain stops in Roanoke. To the west and southwest lie the other great shapers of this region — the mountains. Drive south on Interstate 81 from Roanoke to the university town of Blacksburg. In less than an hour you'll climb several hundred feet in elevation, breaking through the walled east flank of the Appalachians and coming out (right at Exit 37) onto the highland plateau. It's one of the greatest pieces of Interstate in America, especially in the Fall. If you keep going southwest to I-77, and then turn south toward Charlotte, you'll come back down through the wall into the Carolina piedmont on an incline that stretches continuously and sometimes steeply for over twenty miles. Before the Interstate system, that piece of terrain killed dozens of truckers whose brakes couldn't take it. It's still a place to be cautious.

From the mountains comes coal, lots of it. Mining is a tough life, and the people out there are a strong lot. Their coal has heated a lot of homes, made some people rich, and still forms a stable base for the Norfolk Southern's prosperity.

Also from the mountains come springs and turbulent rivers and still-clean lakes, like Claytor, Philpott, and Mountain. The New River (actually, very old, geologically) has some of America's best white water. Fishing is uniformly good. The springs not only watered farms, but tourists as well. Mineral-spring spas were the rage of the 19th century; the theory was anything which tasted and smelled so awful *had* to be good for you. Hollins College was built from a sulphur-sping resort hotel. And springs were the beginning of one of the world's most famous resorts, the Homestead, northwest of Roanoke near the West Virginia line.

Though many of the features of the region can be guessed from the physical setting — great parks, camping, hiking and hunting, for example — one facet sure to surprise an outsider is the vitality of the arts. Though folk arts and crafts are potent, obviously (check out the Blue Ridge Farm Museum at Ferrum, for example), it is the fine arts which catch you unaware. Nearly twenty commercial galleries do a solid business in the Roanoke — Blacksburg — Christiansburg corridor alone. Most area colleges have excellent art programs. Festival-in-the-Park, held in Roanoke's Elmwood Park the first weekend every June, has grown in 25 years from a tiny sidewalk art show into a week-long festival of visual and performing arts. It draws 150,000 people annually. Few areas like this have a professional symphony, let alone a Youth Symphony. Roanoke had both public radio (NPR) and public TV (PBS) before many larger cities did. People from the Blue Ridge to the Tennessee line can curl up with Evening at Pops or the Metropolitan Opera.

So as you stand on the overlook at Mill Mountain, within the city limits of Roanoke itself, try to ignore the old 100-foot illuminated steel star to your right, a monument to civic boosterism that is loved by many and despised by equal numbers. Instead, look out over the city, then northeast up the Valley, then southwest toward the mountains. Reflect on the diversity of it all. If culture in the coalfields and urbanity west of the Piedmont still surprises you, don't feel bad.

I told you, it's one of the best kept secrets in the east.

ROANOKE

Lodging: (703)

Best Western Coachman Inn, I-81, Ex. 44, 992-1234
Blue Jay Motel, Salem, 380-2080
Blue Ridge Motel, 3315 Orange Ave., NE, 343-7384
Cardinal Motel, I-81, Ex. 45, 992-1362
Colony House Motor Lodge, 3560 Franklin Rd., SW, 345-0411
Days Inn of Roanoke, 535 Orange Ave., 342-4551
Econo-Travel of Roanoke, 3816 Franklin Rd. SW, 774-1621
 1535 East Main St., 366-2426
 308 Orange Ave., 343-2413
 6621 Thirlane Rd. NW, 563-0853
Embassy Motor Lodge, 4525 Melrose Ave., 362-1201
Goodwin Motel, Salem, 389-7233
Holiday Inn-Airport, 6626 Thirlane Rd. NW, 366-8861
 Civic Center, Williamson Rd. & Orange Ave., 342-8961
 Salem, I-81, Ex. 40, 389-7061
 South, 1927 Franklin Rd., 343-0121
 Tanglewood, 4368 Starkey Rd., 774-4400
Motel Hollins, Hollins, 992-2971
Howard Johnson Motor Lodge, I-81, Ex. 44, 992-3000
 7656 Williamson Rd., 366-7671
Jefferson Inn, 616 S. Brandon Ave., 342-2951
Lee Hy Auto Court, 3318 Brandon Ave., 342-8429
Monticello Motel, 5046 Williamson Rd., 366-3408
Olympia Inn, 7120 Williamson Rd., 366-7681
Omega Inn, 526 Orange Ave., 981-9341
Parkway Motel, US 220 S, 774-1679
Patrick Henry Hotel, 617 S. Jefferson St., 345-8811
Plantation Motel, 4602 Williamson Rd., 563-1332
Plaza Motel, 4511 Williamson Rd., 366-3441
Ramada Inn, I-81, Ex. 43, 366-0341
Ranch Motel, 2032 W. Main St., 387-1288
Regency Square, 2302 Williamson Rd., 563-2831
Regina Motor Lodge, 2102 W. Main St., 389-7258
Hotel Roanoke, 19 N Jefferson St., 343-6992
Roanoke Tourist Motel, 2968 Orange Ave., 343-2009
Roanoker Motor Lodge, 7645 Williamson Rd., 362-3344
Roma Budget Inn, 4611 Williamson Rd., 362-9200
Salem Motel Court, 1806 W. Main St., 389-3282
Shangri-La Motel, 5125 Williamson Rd., 362-1831
Sheraton-Airport Inn, 2725 Ferndale Dr. NW, 362-4500
 Sheraton-Salem, I-81, Ex. 41, 563-9711
Siesta Motel, 2746 W. Main St., 387-9541
Skyline Motel, US 220 S, 989-9275
Starlite Motor Court, 4448 Melrose Ave., 366-3403

Thrifty Inn, 6520 Thirlane Rd. NW, 563-2871
Town Motel, 2326 Williamson Rd., 366-3372
TraveLodge, 320 Kimball Ave. NE, 344-0981
Traveltown Motel, Cloverdale, 992-1521
Windsor Motel, 1918 W. Main St., 389-5485

Campgrounds: (703)
Church of God Camp Ground, 366-9806
Crazy Horse Campground, 721-2792
Safari Campground, 297-5433
Sun Valley Swim Club & Campground, 343-8766
Whip-O-Will Campground, 297-4459

Dining: (703)
Fast Food
Arbys, 685 Brandon Ave. SW, 342-3292
   5442 Williamson Rd., NW, 362-8127
Burger King, 4815 Williamson Rd., 362-1333
   2626 Franklin Rd, 343-6038
   3216 Melrose Ave. NW, 343-3904
   716 Hardy Rd, 345-4051
   815 W. Main St., 387-1617
   7121 Williamson Rd. NW, 362-2975
Church's Fried Chicken, 2801 Melrose Ave. NW, 981-1713
Dairy Queen, 1608 Peters Creed Rd. NW, 362k-4009
   1300 Washington Ave., 981-1050
Hardee's, 3729 Brambleton Ave. SW, 989-5533
   1255 Electric Rd., 389-6459
   3011 Hershberger Rd. NW, 362-8606
   3406 Hollins Rd. NE, 563-0992
   2301 Orange Ave. NE, 981-1973
   7404 Williamson Rd. NW, 362-5504
Kentucky Fried Chicken, Hardy Rd., 343-8729
   3009 Brambleton Ave. SW, 989-8084
   4101 Melrose Ave. NW, 366-3225
   5209 Williamson Rd. NW, 362-3187
Little Chef Restaurant, 1307 Williamson Rd. NE
Long John Silver's Seafood Shoppe, 2809 Franklin Rd. SW,
   345-4555
   4713 Williamson Rd. NW, 366-7000
   1446 Apperson Dr., 389-5088
   801 Hardy Rd., 344-6393
   1205 W. Main St., 387-3120
   3743 Brambleton Ave. SW, 744-2767
McDonald's, 5436 Williamson Rd. NW, 366-3229
   Lee Hi Shopping Center, 774-6295
   3938 Melrose Ave. NW, 366-2076

```
┌─────────────────────────────────────────────────────┐
│                                                     │
│  IN ROANOKE —    𝒥ppy's                             │
│                                                     │
│           The Finest in Steaks and Salads           │
│                     Since 1919                      │
│                                                     │
│         Live Entertainment — Seating for 400        │
│                     342-7919                        │
│                  2926 Franklin Road                 │
│                                                     │
└─────────────────────────────────────────────────────┘
```

809 Hardy Rd., 345-9291
Civic Center, 342-4007
2801 Franklin Rd. SW, 345-4434
1203 W. Main St., 387-3756
Pizza Hut, 3334 Brambleton Ave. NW, 774-8996
683 Brandon Ave. SW, 343-6444
1016 Hershberger Rd. NW, 362-3834
4005 Melrose Ave. NW, 366-7847
326 Orange Ave. NW, 342-6552
1224 W. Main St., 387-1857
Pizza Inn, 504 E. 4th St., 387-0203
3944 Brambleton Ave. SW, 989-3389
3603 Franklin Rd. SW, 981-1447
7326 Williamson Rd. NW, 362-1219
1000 Hardy Rd., 343-1526
202 Orange Ave. NE, 982-7027
Tastee Freez, Blue Ridge, 977-8648
2069 W. Main St., 389-3210
Texas Tavern, 114 Church Ave. W, 342-4825
Wendy's Old Fashioned Hamburgers, 4032 Avenham Ave. SW,
774-0939
1625 Hershberger Rd. NW, 563-2178
903 W. Main St., 387-0082

Family & Cafeteria
Aunt Fannie's Restaurant, 4824 Williamson Rd. NW, 366-6003
Belle's, US 220 & Franklin Rd., 343-0121
Billy's Barn, Rt. 311, 389-0209
Billy's Ritz, 102 Salem Ave. SE, 342-3937
Bonanza Sirloin Pit, 5515 Williamson Rd. NW, 366-5126
3900 Brambleton Ave. SW, 774-7390
260 Wildwood Rd., 389-2801
Brown Derby Pancake House, 1609 Peters Creek Rd. NW, 563-1259
4405 Williamson Rd. NW, 362-3943
8117 Plantation Rd. NW, 366-1968

3521 Franklin Rd. SW, 343-9702
1021 Orange Ave. NE, 342-3365
813 4th St., SE, 345-5791
Catawaba Emporium, Crossroads Mall, 366-8402
Country Cookin', 4521 Melrose Ave. NW, 986-0440
Dot & Toney's Family Restaurant, 1327 Grandin Rd. SW, 981-1078
Down the Hatch, 617 Jeffferson St., 982-5693
Duff's Famous Smorgasbord, Roanoke Salem Plaza, 362-8743
Fat Man, 19 W. Church St., 345-6616
Golden Corral Family Steak House, Electric Rd. SW, 774-8677
Ground Round, Rt. 419, 989-0998
Guy's, 301 First St. SW, 342-6567
Homeplace, Rt. 311, 384-7252
Howard Johnson's, 7650 Williamson Rd. NW, 362-8200
Jefferson Coffee Shoppe, 616 S. Jefferson St., 342-2951
K & W Cafeteria, Tanglewood Mall, 989-3369
   Crossroads Mall, 563-4977
Mac & Maggie's, Tanglewood Mall, 774-7427
Oasis, 4017 Williamson Rd. NW, 366-0347
Pancake House, 1840 Apperson Dr., 389-6549
Parkside Buffeteria, 2177 Dale Ave. SE, 981-1589
Parlor Days, 311 Day Ave. SW, 344-2713
Pierre's, 7707 Williamson Rd. NW, 362-1600
Richfield Inn, 25 Knollwood Rd., 389-3100
Roadhouse, Tanglewood Mall, 774-0006
Roanoker Restaurant, 2522 Colonial Ave., 344-7746
Roger's Cabin Bar-B-Que, Elm Ave. & Wasena Bridge, 345-3079
Shoney's Big Boy Restaurants, 1808 Hershberger Rd. NW, 366-7734
   3865 Electric Rd., 989-3533
   7629 Williamson Rd. NW, 563-2044
Snuggery, 1436 W. Main St., 389-0317
Soup Kitchen, 102 Franklin Rd., 344-0039
S & S Cafeteria, Towers Mall, 985-0864
T J's Restaurant, 1340 Washngton Ave., 345-4535
Top Rail, 1106 Kessler Mill Rd., 389-0917
Wayne's, 1211 Fourth St. SW, 982-9045
Western Sizzlin', Williamson Rd. & Orange Ave., 342-6403
   3830 Franklin Rd. SW, 989-4675
Wilson's, 3109 Brambleton Ave. SW, 774-1199
Ye Olde English Inn, Rt. 221, 774-2670

Delicatessen
B R Guest Delicatessen, 210-B 1st St. SE, 982-1131
Crystal Spring Deli, 2221 Crystal Spring Ave., 345-1276
Gerow's Restaurant & Deli, 4301 Brambleton Ave. SW, 774-1442
Good Shepherd Inn, 18 E. Campbell Ave., 344-6316
International Gourmet, Towers Shopping Center, 344-8960

Johnny D's Deli, 1342 Riverland Rd. SE, 342-4463
Jumbo's Subs & Pizzá, Oak Grove Plaza, 774-1555
Mac & Bob's Deli, 316 E. Main St. 389-5999
Macado's, 111 Church Ave. SW, 342-7231
Mike's Deli & Lounge, 16 W. Kirk Ave., 343-7000
Nature's Deli Delight, 29 Kirk Ave. SW, 345-5045
New Yorker Delicatessen & Restaurant, 2802 Williamson Rd.,
    342-0935
Newby's Delicatessen, 3720 Franklin Rd. SW, 342-9655
Ninth St. Pizza & Sub Shop, 1132 9th St. SW, 982-9798
Pete's Delikatessen & Snack Shoppe, Crossroads Shopping Mall,
    563-2851
Pizza & Hoagie House, 206 Apperson Dr., 387-9636
Salem Pizza & Hoagie, 1 W. Main St., 389-7622

Surf & Turf
Aquarium, 3369 Shenandoah Ave. NW, 982-1610
B F Goodribs, 2824 Franklin Rd. SW, 342-9482
Bogart's Restaurant, 3121 Franklin Rd. SW, 342-7693
Charcoal Steak House, 5225 Williamson Rd. NW, 366-3710
C J's Steak & Seafood, 3503 Williamson Rd. SW, 981-1376
Coach & Four, 5206 Williamson Rd. NW, 362-4220
Family Fish House, 7416 Williamson Rd., 362-4813
Flaming Pit, I-81 & Plantation Rd., 366-0341
Harbor's Landing, 5610 Williamson Rd. NW, 362-8233
Market Place Oyster Bar, 312 First St. SE, 345-6677
Omar's, 1455 Spartan Square, 389-1587
Parker's Seafood Kitchen, 1336 Peters Creek Rd. NW, 362-3900
Parkway Restaurant, Rt. 220S, 774-7691
Reb Lobster, 3525 Franklin Rd. SW, 342-1549
Shucker's, 30 Church St. SE, 981-0000
Steak & Ale, Avenham at Tanglewood Mall, 774-0071
T-Bone Charlie's, 3655 Brambleton Ave. SW, 989-4955
That Seafood Place, I-81, Ex. 41, 362-4211

Chinese & Oriental
Chinese Pagoda Restaurant, 4513 Williamson Rd. NW, 563-1636
Fiji Island Restaurant, 627 Townside Rd. SW, 343-2552
House of Hunan, 4115 Melrose Ave. NW, 563-4827
Kabuki Japanese Steak House, 3503 Williamson Rd. SW, 981-0222
Kim Tiki Restaurant, 4115 Melrose Ave. NW, 366-1324
Mandarin House Restaurant, 3566 Franklin Rd. SW, 344-4351
Matsuri of Japan, 4325 Brambleton Ave. SW, 989-9129
Peking China House, W. Salem Plaza, 389-1433
Peking Palace Restaurant, 4414 Melrose Ave. NW, 563-1296
Shanghai Restaurant, 219 Apperson Dr., 389-4151

Italian

Carini Pizza & Restaurant, 4913 Grandin Rd. SW, 989-8670
D J's Brasserie Restaurant, Tanglewood Mall, 774-8694
Ferro's Pizza & Restaurant, 5524 Williamson Rd. NW, 563-9776
Jarbas Italian Gourmet, 4120 Franklin Rd. SW, 774-5274
Luigi's Italian Gourmet Restaurant, 3301 Brambleton Ave. SW, 989-6277
Patricia's, 3505 Franklin Rd. SW, 342-4641
Paulo's Restaurant & Lounge, 5236 Williamson Rd. NW, 563-2260
Roberto's, 3505 Franklin Rd., 342-4641
Roma Restaurant, 4611 Williamson Rd. NW, 366-2691
11 Walnut Ave. SW, 345-0047
Villa Sorrento Restaurant, 1210 Patterson AVe. SW, 342-2524

Mexican

Fiesta Cantina, 3805 Melrose Ave. NW, 362-9227
2133 Franklin Rd. SW, 342-9603
Tippy's Taco House, 5528 Williamson Rd. NW, 362-5222

International

Ad Lib, 19 Jefferson St. N, 343-6992
Alexander's, 125 E. Campbell Ave. 982-6983
Berkeley's Top of the Town, I-81, Ex. 41, 563-9711
Canopy Restaurant, 3121 Franklin Rd., 343-0000
Charley's, Grand Pavilion, 774-7475
Elephant Walk, Starkey Rd. & Hwy 419, 774-4400
Fesquet's, Crossroads Mall, 362-8803
Four Parrots, 617 Jefferson St. 342-1295
Hotel Roanoke Regency Room, 19 N. Jefferson St., 343-6992
La Maison du Gourmet, 5732 Airport Rd., 366-2444
Oscar's, 2727 Ferndale Dr. NW, 362-4500
P Capers, 7512 Williamson Rd. NW, 362-9244

Dinner Theatre

Barn Dinner Theatre, 6071 Airport Rd. NW, 362-3333

ROANOKE

Potpourri

The city's population exceeds 100,000 with an estimated population for the metro area at about 230,000. The elevation here stands at 945 feet. Roanoke is located in the western part of the state. We would think that it would be safe in referring to it as the "Gateway to Southwest Virginia."

Climate is generally in keeping with the surrounding area. There are four seasons with some very hot days in summer and likewise cold ones in winter. Rainfall is about 40 inches per year with snow at about 25.

The transportation situation for visitors to the area is excellent. Woodrum Field, the local airport, offers scheduled air service by Piedmont Airlines as well as commuter service provided by Air Virginia and others.

Roanoke has long been known as a railroad town in that it was the home for the Norfolk & Western Railroad. Now, it is the recently merged Norfolk & Southern. Greyhound and Trailways provide bus service. From the standpoint of the motorist entry and egress is a simple matter. I-81 is tied in to the city by I-581. US 11 parallels I-81. US Highways 220, 221, and 460 connect the city to other destinations.

Roanoke prides itself for the distinction of having been designated an All American City some three times in recent years.

History
Roanoke is considered to be in the Roanoke Valley. This can be considered an extension of the Shenandoah Valley. It was first explored in 1671. Early settlers from eastern Virginia and Pennsylvania began cultivating this rich soil in 1740.

Local history is so closely involved by changing names for the same locale. There is a history of towns being formed from various subdivisions. There is also the evolution of the various counties in the region. It was in the early part of the 19th Century that what today is the City of Roanoke was formed. The pedigree goes back to such place names as Antwerp followed by Gainesborough and thence Old Lick. It was in 1874 that the Town of Big Lick was chartered. It was a city of 500 people which in 1882 became the Town of Roanoke. In 1884 it was finally to receive its present designation: City of Roanoke.

The city was located on what were the tracks for the Atlantic, Mississippi and Ohio Railroad. This was to become the Norfolk & Western and finally the Norfolk & Southern. It is obvious that the evolution of change results in the adoption of new names. But, it is so important to realize that the forward progress of Roanoke came about as the result of growth and prosperity for the N & W (as it is affectionately referred to by locals).

Education
HOLLINS COLLEGE — This is a well known private college for women located in nearby Hollins, Virginia. Enrollment is about 975.

ROANOKE COLLEGE — Situated in nearby Salem, Virginia, this coeducational college has an enrollment of about 1400.

UNIVERSITY OF VIRGINIA EXTENSION — Locally handles about 3800.

VIRGINIA WESTERN COMMUNITY COLLEGE — Two year college in the state system of community colleges has an enrollment of about 5500.

NATIONAL BUSINESS COLLEGE — A private school with an enrollment of about 1000.

FERRUM COLLEGE — Located in Ferrum, Virginia, some 10 miles west of Rocky Mount, Virginia. This is a liberal arts college offering majors in 25 areas. This is a coeducational college with an enrollment of 1500. It is a Methodist Church related institution offering two year Associate as well as four year bachelor degree programs. It is interesting to note that during the summer the College provides accommodations and recreational facilities for vacationers. Further information: Ferrum College, Ferrum, VA 24088, 703/365-2121.

Nearby schools are Radford University and Virginia Polytechnic Institute and State University.

Sightseeing
MILL MOUNTAIN PARK — At 2000 feet elevation this park overlooks the City of Roanoke as well as the Roanoke and Shenandoah Valleys. The view is worth the trip. Don't discount the night view — really romantic. Daytime activities on Mill Mountain can include a visit to the miniature train and children's zoo. The latter contains a collection of small animals in nursery rhyme motif. This is a good place for picnics. A three mile spur connects the Mountain with the Blue Ridge Parkway.

TRANSPORTATION MUSEUM — This is one that the kids will enjoy. Located in Wasena Park is this collection of steam locomotives and other type vehicles.

LAKESIDE AMUSEMENT PARK — The kids will really love this 60 acre facility. There are plenty of rides as well as picnic facilities. Generally, there is country and western entertainment on Saturday nights with Sundays earmarked for families. Open April to end of August. There are weekend dates in September.

DIXIE CAVERNS — Located five miles west of Salem are these very interesting caverns. Picnic and camping facilities here.

SMITH MOUNTAIN LAKE — This 22,000 acre lake has become the recreational center of this part of the state. Located about 30 miles from Roanoke this facility has provided many hours of enjoyment for property owners and individuals availing themselves of privately owned facilities. Recently, a state park has been opened which provides public access.

BOOKER T. WASHINGTON NATIONAL MONUMENT — Located 20 miles southeast of Roanoke via Va. 116S and Va. 122N. We suggest that you begin at the Visitor Center which contains exhibits on Washington's life and an audio visual program interpreting his career and accomplishments. Following the trip to the Visitors Center travel the Plantation Trail and become acquainted with the environment that helped shape the character of this renowned educator.

FARMER'S MARKET — Located in the heart of Roanoke's main business district is this restored area which began in 1874. You will find this to be a continental experience in the mountains of Virginia. This offers a completely unique blend of shopping with its many galleries, shops, and restaurants.

CENTER IN THE SQUARE — Now, as we write this piece, the finishing touches are being put to this $10 million dollar project scheduled to open in December, 1983. This cultural capitol will house the Museum of Fine Arts, The Museum of Science (including a planetarium), The Mill Mountain Playhouse, The Roanoke Valley Historical Society, and The Roanoke Valley Arts Council. The latter will have a visitor information center. This fabulous center will be at the Farmers Market at Campbell & First Streets. Further information: Center In The Square, 201 First St., SE, Roanoke, VA 24011, 703/344-1418.

INFORMATION — Roanoke Valley Convention & Visitors Bureau, 14 W. Kirk Avenue, Roanoke, VA 24011, 703/344-5188.

CIVIC CENTER — A multi purpose facility housing a coliseum-arena, a fully equipped auditorium-theater, and a versatile exhibit-assembly hall.

Some More Things To Do

ROANOKE SYMPHONY ORCHESTRA — A full season. Further information: Call Symphony Office, 703/343-9127.

SHOWPLACE AT THE BARN — Dinner theater. Contact: 6071 Airport Road, Roanoke, VA 24012, 703/362-3333.

SALEM REDBIRDS — Minor league baseball team playing in nearby Salem, Virginia.

FESTIVAL WEEK — This is a gala week held annually during the early part of June in which numerous free events are enjoyed by the public. The festival brings artists and performers together for a celebration of life and the arts. It's a real fun time for the community with activities and food for all. Further information: Festival, P.O. Box 8276, Roanoke, VA 24014, 703/342-2640.

BLUE RIDGE INSTITUTE — Dedicated to the preservation of Blue Ridge cultural heritage it was organized as a division of Ferrum College in the 1970's. The institute is committed to the research, preservation, documentation and communication of the traditional life and culture of the Blue Ridge Mountains. The visitor is able to visit the Blue Ridge Farm Museum. This is an authentic working reproduction of an 1800 German farm. It is representative of the early Blue Ridge settlements. Under construction is a 1900 farm which illustrates the scene as the area became further settled.

Visitors will also be able to learn of the recordings produced by the Institute during the past five years. There is a sampling of regional music from both vintage and recent years. In addition, radio and television documentaries have been produced disseminating information on Virginia folk practices and traditions. The Blue Ridge Heritage Archive houses countless materials on the history and culture of Virginia and the Blue Ridge Region.

There is a craft shop here that promotes the work of local craftspersons through sale of their goods. Admission charge.

BLUE RIDGE FOLK LIFE FESTIVAL — This annual celebration of traditional mountain music, crafts, food, and recreation is held on the Ferrum College campus annually on the fourth Saturday in October. Admission charge.

Further information both BRI and the Festival may be secured from: Blue Ridge Institute, Ferrum College, Ferrum, VA 24088, 703/365-2121x107.

THE BLUE RIDGE INSTITUTE
AT FERRUM COLLEGE

By Roderick Moore, Director, Blue Ridge Institute

The Blue Ridge Institute is committed to the research, preservation, documentation and communication of the traditional life and culture of the Blue Ridge Mountains. In all of our programs and activities the emphasis is on the development of an understanding and appreciation of the history and folkways of this important region.

The Institute was organized in the early 1970's as a division of Ferrum College, which has a long history of serving the rural people of the mountain region. Courses are offered through the College in Virginia folklife and folk music, in addition to less formal workshops using the resources of the Blue Ridge Farm Museum and the Ferrum Craft Shop.

The Blue Ridge region was penetrated by English and Scotch-Irish colonists from eastern Virginia and by German settlers moving south from Pennsylvania through the Shenandoah Valley, starting in the 1750's. The legacy of these pioneers can still be found in the material and oral culture of the mountains today; the forms of buildings and furniture, the sounds of music, the skills of craftworkers, the traditional foods, and the stories, legends and beliefs that still circulate. The mission of the Blue Ridge Institute is to record and interpret this rich culture, thereby helping to enhance the quality of life and promote the responsible development of the Blue Ridge.

The Blue Ridge Farm Museum presents the history of the mountain region through reconstructed farmsteads and living history programs. The 1800 German farm consists of a log house and kitchen, a bank barn, a garden and outbuildings representative of the early settlements by pioneers moving south along the Blue Ridge mountain chain. Presently under construction is a 1900 farm illustrating the adaptations and cultural sharing that occurred as the region became more settled. All of the farm buildings are authentic to the time period and region and have been moved from their original locations to the museum site. Plants and crops of the time are being raised, and costumed interpreters perform farm and household chores based on research into daily life and customs in early Virginia.

Held every year in October on the Ferrum College campus, the Blue Ridge Folklife Festival offers visitors demonstrations and performances of traditional mountain skills and crafts. The day-long event features musical performances, craftsworkers, preparation and sales

An 1800 German farmstead at Ferrum College's Blue Ridge Farm Museum

of regional foods, horse and mule pulling contests, steam and gas engine demonstrations, children's games, coon dog contests and an exhibit of the region's car culture.

An exhibit from the museum's permanent collection called "Living Traditions: Traditional Crafts of the Blue Ridge," is displayed in the exhibit room in the BRI building. The objects include baskets, pottery, toys, musical instruments, textiles, woodcarvings and leatherwork, all of which were made with traditional skills and materials by contemporary artisans and are part of the Institute's ongoing collecting of the works of living traditional craftspersons.

The BRI's school programs include numerous presentations of the region's folk culture to encourage awareness of an interest in local traditions. They are now expanding to include tours and living history workshops at the Farm Museum coordinated with local school curricula.

Since 1978 BRI Records has been producing a series on "Virginia Traditions," presenting performances of regional music from both vintage and recent recordings. Vocal and instrumental pieces are featured from such diverse traditions as balladry, blues, native Virginia songs, piano music, work songs and storytelling. Each album has been thoroughly researched and includes a booklet of analytic and descriptive notes on the music and the performers.

In disseminating information on Virginia folk practices and traditions, the BRI has produced a number of radio and television documentaries. Working with both public and commercial broadcasters, programs have been presented on many types of music, local musicians, foodways and crafts. Two series are available for public presentation: eight videocassettes on "Virginia's Back-Country Museums," documenting lesser-known historic museums in western Virginia; and 26 hour-long radio programs on "Traditional Music in Virginia," covering religious, bluegrass, ballad and stringband music, regional performance styles, early influential performers and storytelling.

The Blue Ridge Heritage Archive houses a collection of documentary materials on the history and cultures of Virginia and the Blue Ridge region. The Archive's audio tapes, records, photographs, manuscripts, books and videotapes contain information on traditional music, crafts, foodways, belief system, agricultural practices and ways of life. Of particular importance are several special collections including the Earl Palmer Photograph Collection, the Elmer Smith Collection of Shenandoah Valley folklore, the James Taylor Adams Manuscript Collection of tales and songs, and the Carter-Owen Tape Collection of music from the Virginia-North Carolina border area of the Blue Ridge Mountains. The Archive resources are available for study and research by arrangement with the BRI.

The Ferrum Craft Shop promotes the work of local craftspersons through sales of their goods and through educational workshops and programs. Handcrafted items for sale include woodcarvings, quilts, tinware, pottery, toys, weavings, and baskets; art and craft supplies are also available. Workshops in traditional crafts are sponsored by the Craft Shop as well, taught by community artisans.

Highland Maple Festival, Monterey

INTERMODAL TRAVEL

Travel patterns have changed over the years. At one time man got from one place to the next on foot. Today man has become more advanced in this business of getting from place to place. Suffice to say, we have reached a relatively more sophisticated means of getting around today than did the American Indian that earlier inhabited western Virginia.

Our choice of transportation forms can depend on various factors. We may be concerned with the condition of our pocketbook. Maybe it's our own physical condition that is the governing factor. On the other hand, we may be concerned with the availability of time. Maybe it is convenience or maybe it is attention to the development of an efficient trip. It is possible that our decision was based on a combination of those and other factors. On the other hand, it is also very possible that we never gave the matter a second thought and are operating by "the seat of our pants." In short, the possibility exists that we are creatures of habit that gave little thought to the whole question of — form of travel.

All that we wish to do in this article is to challenge you to consider the possible use of intermodal travel for your visit to western Virginia. It might make for an even better trip for all in your party.

Let us relate to the business of visiting this specific area of Virginia. Assume that a couple comes here from London or Madrid. It is doubtful that they are going to ship their car from Europe in order to complete their one week visit of western Virginia. The cost could prove to be prohibitive. Their solution is quite easily obvious. They could fly to Dulles Airport. From here they can rent a car and thoroughly take in all of the sights in this "target area." They can set their own pace — they can see what they want and by the same token pass up that which does not appeal. But, when it is all over they will have seen the true U.S. from the "grass roots" level. Not to be forgotten is the fact that this could prove to be a very economical and efficient way to learn and enjoy at first hand. They terminate their visit at the same airport and return to Europe. They also have the option of continuing to another airport where they drop off the car and fly to another region.

Let us now consider the couple that lives on the west coast. They are intent on visiting western Virginia but have no desire to drive across the country. Their solution is so apparent. They fly from the "coast" to say Dulles. Here, they pick up their car rental and embark on their total visitation. They circle as much of the target area as they can plus other possible areas. Then, they return to their starting point where they drop off the car and board their plane for home.

We have mentioned Dulles Airport as a point of entry. Maybe, we should in fairness say Airport X as there are so many other options. Maybe the couple doesn't want to commence their visitation in the northern part of the state. They could readily change planes in Washington and fly into Charlottesville where they could pick up a car there. It is possible that they might fly in to Atlanta from the west coast and connect with a flight to Roanoke. It is here that they could start their car rental. The beauty of this system is the flexibility that is afforded to the traveler. It's efficient and cost effective.

The air traveler is not restricted as to choice of airport. Trunk and commuter carriers carry passengers to airports of all size. Car rental companies can be found at most airports in the country. Many car rental companies base themselves in the nearby towns or cities. They are often no more than a stone's throw from the airport.

Intermodal is just a fancy word to describe the ability to travel on more than one mode of transport. In the strict sense, it is going from one form of travel to another in order to arrive at a desired travel objective.

Why not consider the financial savings that you can realize by combining various forms of transportation on your visit to this region. You might even consider combining Amtrak with your own car rental. Certainly, Amtrak offers the ability to go from one downtown center to another in an expeditious manner without resort to round trip airport transfers. In many instances the economy is obvious. In case of family travel, you might find that the children will be thrilled at their first train ride.

Never to be forgotten is the wear and tear on both car and driver when you traverse great distances in your own car. The efficiency and cost savings can well be your reward for trying the intermodal option.

— Warren Evans

GEOLOGY FORMED THE FACE OF WESTERN VIRGINIA

By George E. Beetham, Jr.

The face of western Virginia is wrinkled with age — a corrugated washboard made up of mountains and valleys.

The geography of the area, though not anywhere near as rugged as the Rockies in the West, has had a decided effect on settlement and travel. You sometimes have to drive many miles in order to reach a place only a few miles distant, and maybe drive a narrow, twisting mountain road to accomplish the task.

But there are rewards. The mountain scenery can be breathtaking, and western Virginia has many panoramic views to offer.

The geology that makes up the mountainous terrain varies from the volcanic rock of the Blue Ridge to the seafloor sediments of the Alleghenies. These mountains are old — more than a billion years old in the Blue Ridge and around Mt. Rogers, Virginia's highest peak at 5,729 feet, in the southwestern part of the state.

In the older volcanic rocks lie metallic minerals and gemstones, while the somewhat younger sedimentary rocks to the west — checking in at less than 400 million years old — offer fossil impressions of ancient sea creatures, bog plants and land animals.

The geologic history of the area began with volcanic action in what is now the Blue Ridge. What may have been an island chain of volcanic fissures built up deposits of lava. Heat and pressure compressed the lava, which has become a greenish basalt-like rock known as greenstone.

The mountains that built up from lava flows eroded; rocks, sand and soil washed into an ancient sea. The deposits built up on the seafloor, along with shells of sea creatures, and were packed tightly on the bed. Shifts in the Earth's crust forced those deposits to fold and be lifted up, creating new mountains. The process of erosion, sedimentation and uplift may have gone on for some time, creating different mountains and different seas.

Sea life was preserved in fossil form when shells and skeletal remains were deposited on the floor of the sea, while land life became carbonized in fossil form. Coal, oil and natural gas are some of the fossil forms now used for fuels.

The geologic past is responsible for Virginia's natural resources as well as her beautiful vistas and transportation routes.

As you travel the scenic byways and mountain routes, you will find many attractions carved by nature — mountain overlooks, waterfalls, caverns, natural bridges, tunnels, spires and chimneys —formed by the geologic process of earth formation.

You will notice the effect of the terrain on settlement and development. The rolling farmland of the Shenandoah Valley was settled from the north by Germans and Scotch-Irish from Pennsylvania, while areas to the immediate east of the Blue Ridge were settled primarily by English moving westward from the seacoast.

The Blue Ridge acted as a mountain barrier, and the result is demonstrated in subtle differences in architecture between regions.

In the narrow valleys of the Alleghenies, even farms are crowded by the steep slopes of mountains. Settlement there was sparse; towns are few.

If you ask a Virginian about geology or settlement, chances are that you'll get a puzzled look. But if you ask the same person what they think about the state, they'll most likely tell you there's no place on Earth they'd rather be.

The mountains of western Virginia offer a variety of recreational opportunities. Hunting, fishing, camping, hiking, backpacking, simple picnics or auto touring are just some of the outdoor things available.

Within Virginia are the George Washington and Jefferson National Forests, where all of those pursuits can be indulged.

Shenanodah National Park and the Blue Ridge Parkway offer just about everything but hunting. There is the 105-mile long Skyline Drive in Shenandoah National Park, where deer can be seen at dawn and dusk, grazing along the drive or in meadows.

Both the parkway and drive offer colorful vistas when the leaves turn in October, reaching the peak of color about mid-month.

Sometimes, when taking in a picturesque scene, it's not too hard to get the notion that all of the earth-history that formed what you're looking at took place just for you.

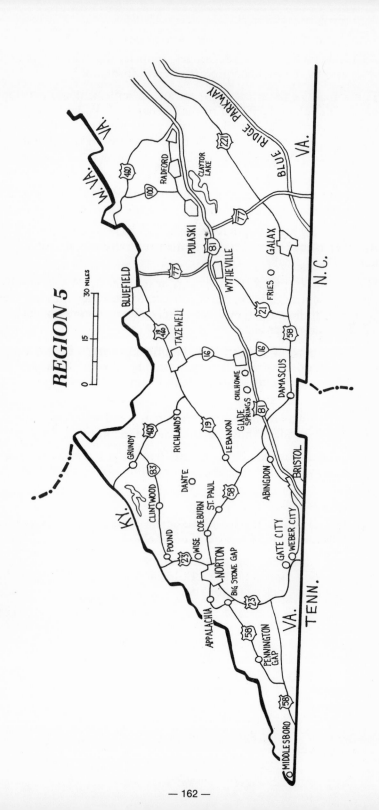

REGION 5

0   15   30 MILES

ABINGDON

Lodgings: (703)
Alpine Motel, I-81, Ex. 9, 628-3178
Empire Motor Lodge, I-81, Ex. 9, 628-7131
Glade Economy Inn, I-81, Ex. 11, Glade Spring, 429-5131
Howard Johnson's Motor Lodge, I-81, Ex. 5, Bristol, 669-1151
Inn Towner Motor Court, 804 W. Main, 628-3115
Martha Washington Inn, I-81, Ex. 8, 628-3161
Shamrock Motor Lodge, I-81, Ex. 5, 669-4148
Shiloh Motor Lodge, Rt. 19, 1 mil. N., 628-7106
Skyland Motel, I-81, Ex. 5, Bristol, 669-0166

Restaurants: (703)
Bella's Pizza, I-81, Ex. 9, 628-8101
Betty's Party House, Rt. 11, 944-3261, Reservations Required
Big "T" Family Restaurant, Hwy. 19, 628-5165
Burger King, I-81, Ex. 9, 628-8770
Cisso's, 509 E. Main St., 628-4611
Empire Restaurant, I-81, Ex. 9, 628-6131
George's Restaurant, 804 W. Main, 628-3115
Glade Economy Restaurant, Glade Spring, I-81, Ex. 11, 429-5131
The Hardware Company Rest., 260W, Main St., 628-1111
House of Hunan, Bristol, I-81 & 11 W, 764-1444
Kentucky Fried Chicken, I-81, Ex. 8, 628-7201
Long John Silver's Seafood Shopp, I-81, Ex. 8, 628-7432
Mama's Pizza, Wolf Hills Shopping Ctr., 628-4107
Martha Washington's Inn Rest., Main St., 628-3161
Matt's Place, E. Main St., 628-4402
McDonald's, I-81, Ex. 8, 628-6242
Pizza Hut, I-81, Ex. 8, 628-3022
P. J. Brown & Co., 414 E. Main, 628-4111
Plum Alley Eatery, 301 E. Main, 628-8382
S & S Cafeteria, Rt. 19, 628-7179
Shoney's, I-81, Ex. 8, 628-2555
Smokehouse Bar B-Q, I-81, Ex. 9, 628-7755
Southland Restaurant, Bristol, I-81, Ex. 5, 466-2411
Stuckey's Pecan Shoppe, I-81, Ex. 8, 628-3801
Sub Station, 305 W. Main, 628-4822
Tommy's Restaurant, 455 W. Main, 628-7100
Western Steer Family Steak House, I-81, Ex. 9, 628-6621

Campgrounds
Lakeshore, 628-5394
Riverside Family, 628-5333
Washington County Park, 628-9677
Wolf Lair Village

Recreation

A 55 acre tract on the shoreline of the South Holston Lake known as the Washington County Park offers camping, picnicking, and includes an olympic size swimming pool. The park is about nine miles from town. Incidentally, a short six block walk through town will take you back into the 19th century, rewarding the visitor with the ambience of a gentler era. This walk will include a view of the famed Barter Theater where a full schedule of productions is maintained — 628-3991 or 628-2281.

THE WASHINGTON COUNTY PARK is a 55 acre recreation center on the shoreline of South Holston Lake. There are camping and picnic facilities as well as an olympic size swimming pool.

MOUNT ROGERS NATIONAL RECREATION AREA is 154,000 acres of unspoiled woodlands. Excellent for hiking, camping, cross country skiing, horseback riding, and fishing.

GRAYSON HIGHLANDS STATE PARK adjacent to Mt. Rogers National Recreation Area is one of the state's finest — great for outdoor activities.

During the first two weeks of August the Virginia Highlands Art & Crafts Festival is held. It is a real fun affair with an antique flea market, drama, art, crafts, music, folk dancing — don't pass it up.

THE BURLEY TOBACCO FESTIVAL is held in October. Crafts, tobacco, and livestock are displayed and named headliners perform for Country Music shows at night.

In case you note a high mountain be assured that it is Mt. Rogers, the highest in Virginia standing 5729 feet high.

Agriculture is the principal industry.

Sightseeing
A walking tour of the historic section of Abingdon would be a pleasant way to be carried back into the 18th and 19th Centuries. It is a short span of about four blocks in which such graceful buildings as the Martha Washington Inn, and the Cave House can be seen. Not to be forgotten is the famed Barter Theater which is on this walk. Why not escape from today's hustle and bustle and explore this touch of yesteryear? On your walk make certain that you take special note of the Barter Theater and the Cave House Craft Shop. the theater dates back to the depression. It provide unemployed Broadway actors with work and at the same time permitted patrons to view good theater for the contribution of food. There are daily performances excepting Monday from April to October. You can secure further detals by calling: 703/628-3991.

THE CAVE HOUSE CRAFT HOUSE is a cooperative marketing agency for area craftsmen.

Outside of town visit White's Mill, a restored working mill and not to be forgotten, visit the Martha Washington Inn, This former girl's college is furnished in original antiques.

If you have an interest in the manufacturing of pottery, a visit to nearby Damascus will take you to Iron Mountain Stoneware.

Transportation
Abingdon is approximately 32 miles northeast of the Tri-City Airport (Bristol, VA.-TN). The principal air carrier serving that airport is Piedmont Airlines. Greyhound serves Abingdon by land. Motorists will find that I-81 comes to the area's front door.

Shopping

CAVE HOUSE CRAFT SHOP — Operated by Holston Mountain Arts & Crafts co-op, a non-profit marketing agency serving local craftsmen. The shop is located on Main Street and may prove beneficial in picking up that special gift.

DIXIE POTTERY — Located on US 11 approximately three miles west of town. Here you will find pottery, glassware, baskets, and gifts.

IRON MOUNTAIN STONEWARE — Pottery factory between Damascus, Virginia, and Mountain City, Tennessee. Manufacturing of the stoneware items can be viewed. There is a retail store connected with the factory.

WHITE'S MILL — Five miles northeast of Abingdon. This restored mill is interesting to view while in operation. Visitors are able to purchase water-ground products.

Geographical

Abingdon virtually touches the neighboring State of Tennessee. The town is located off I-81 in the southwest part of the Commonwealth of Virginia. Population runs about 4300 persons. The city is part of Washington County. This county is 40 miles east of Kingsport, Tennessee and 130 miles west of Roanoke, Virginia. The county's population is about 47,000. The elevation is 2265 feet and there is a moderate climate complete with the normal four seasons of year.

— Virginia State Travel Service
Working Mill open to Blue Ridge Parkway visitors South of Roanoke

BLUEFIELD
Lodgings:
The Brier Red Carpet Inn, US 460S, 325-9111
Holiday Inn, Cumberland Rd., 325-5421
Sheraton Inn, US 52 & US 460, 325-6170

POTPOURRI
Once again we have a situation where there are two towns of the same name in two adjoining states. In this case it is Virginia and West Virginia. The Virginia town has a population of about 6000 with adjoining Tazewell County having about 50,000. On the West Virginia side the town has approximately 16,000 and Mercer County has about 75,000.

The community refers to itself as being "Nature's Air Conditioned City." There are four seasons here with moderate temperatures for each corresponding part of the year. Rainfall and snowfall runs in excess of 40 inches each per year. The elevation here will run about 2500 feet in both towns. The surrounding mountains will range from 2500 to 4700 feet.

The principal highways serving the area are I-77, US 52 and US 460. The distance from Charleston, W. Va. is 108 miles while Roanoke is some 100 miles away. There is commuter air service from the local Mercer County Airport to Pittsburgh, Charleston, and Roanoke. This same airport offers chartered service as well. Individuals can of course commence their air flights from either Roanoke or Charleston. The Norfolk & Southern Railroad serves this community.

Bluefield State College and Concord College number among some of the area's institutions of higher learning.

BLUEFIELD ART & CRAFTS CENTER, INC. — The center has been designed to present a setting for area artists, craftsmen and related retailers. The center is housed in the "Old City Hall" which is on the National Register of Historic Places. Located at 500 Bland Street.

POCAHONTAS, VA. — This town has a colorful past and was the center for the famous Pocahontas Coalfield. It is the oldest mining town in the world. Its first mine was opened in 1882.

EXHIBITION MINE — This is undoubtedly one of the most unique touristic attractions around. It is operated by the town of Pocahontas. It was first opened to the public in 1938. It is the only coal mine in the world through which visitors may walk or drive their car to view coal that was formed 400,000,000 years ago. Famed Pocahontas #3 Coal Seam which is more than 10 feet in thickness may be seen in its original state. The interior is well lighted and visitors are able to see how coal is cut, blasted, and loaded into mine cars. The mine is open to the public from May 1st until October 31st from 10 AM until 5 PM. It is open daily.

ST. ELIZABETH'S CATHOLIC CHURCH — Founded in 1892 and named in honor of the Patron Saint of Hungary, this beautiful church has a ceiling and back altar with 10 life sized hand painted murals.

POCAHONTAS BAPTIST CHURCH — This historic church was built in 1882.

OPERA HOUSE — Built in 1895; has been restored and is open to the public.

LOG SCHOOL HOUSE — Built in 1884 for the Episcopalians of Pocahontas.

DINNER THEATER — This has been opened for almost four years. Further information may be secured from Historic Pocahontas, Inc., Pocahontas, VA 24635.

Pocahontas is located some nine miles from Bluefield, Virginia.

BRISTOL
Lodgings: (703)   TN (615)
Camara Inn, Tri-City Arpt., Blountville, TN., 323-4155
Econo Travel Motor Hotel, 912 Commonwealth, 466-2112
Heart of Bristol Motor Inn, Euclid Ave., 669-7191
Holiday Inn I-81, I-81 & 11W, 968-1101
Holiday Inn West, Euclid Ave., & W. State, 669-7171
Best Western Regency Inn, Hwy. 11W, 968-9119
Sandman Motel, Abingdon Hwy., 669-3151

Restaurants
Arby's Roast Beef, Lee Hwy., 466-2072
Athens Steak House, 105 Goodson St., 466-8271
The Barn Restaurant, Hwy. 11W, TN, 968-5433
Burger King, 125 Blountville Hwy., TN, 968-2025
    1397 Volunteer Pkwy, TN, 764-1971
    1967 Lee Hwy., VA, 466-8081
Captain D's, 101 Blountville Hwy, TN, 968-7878
    1234 Volunteer Pkwy, TN, 968-3727
Duff's Smorgasbord, 821 Commonwealth, VA 466-4532
The Duffer's Club, Tri-City G & C Club, Blountville, 323-3762
Gregg's Pizza, Parkway Plaza, TN, 968-3129
Hardee's, 1375 Lee Hwy, VA 466-9144
    Volunteer Pkwy, TN, 968-9265
House of Hunan, The Barn Hwy, 11W, TN, 764-1444

McDonald's, 133 Blountville, Hwy, TN, 968-2821
Peach Tree, 1021 Commonwealth Ave., 466-9542
Piccadilly Cafeteria, Bristol Mall, VA, 466-9342
Shoney's, New Kingsport Hwy., TN, 764-5101
The Vinyard Rest., Gate City Hwy.
Wendy's, 110 Blountville Hwy., TN, 968-4811
    Volunteer Pkwy., TN, 968-5512
Western Sizzlin', 609 Gate City Hwy., VA, 466-9144
Wooden Nickel, Volunteer Pkwy., TN, 968-3211

Recreation

Five miles southeast of the city are Bristol Caverns. Beautiful formations and a well executed tour makes it quite worthwhile.

Swimming, waterskiing, fishing, and boating at the South Holston Lake — the lake was created by the South Holston Dam and is considered to be the largest earth-filled dam in the world.

Cherokee National Park is south of Bristol.

More scenic areas can be found at the National Forest.

Music lovers will want to be here in mid-October for the Southeastern Band Festival complete with 8000 musicians representing high school bands from seven states.

Race fans find this to be the place to visit for it is the home of the Bristol International Raceway and Bristol International Dragway. The 500-lap Winston Cup and Busch 500 take place here along with the Winston Spring Nationals, site of the world's richest drag races.

Historical Spots

PEMBERTON OAK — Rallying point at Battle of King's Mountain — the oak is more than 30 feet around at the base.

410 STATE STREET — Site of the first Country Music Recording for national distribution.

SHELBY'S FORT — Dates back fo 1771.

DEERY'S INN — (Blountville) Well preserved Inn established in 1786.

ROCKY MOUNT — The original capitol of Tennessee in 1769. This is the birthplace of "Tennessee" Ernie Ford.

ACUFF CHAPEL — The first Methodist Church west of the Appalachians dates back to 1768.

FORT WOMACK — Residence-fort built in 1774.

EDWARD COX HOUSE — This log home built in 1774.

Cultural

One should not feel that the finer things in life are to be monopolized by the metropolitan areas of the world. There is also a mistaken belief on the part of some visitors to this region that the inhabitants are still living in the 18th Century.

Theatre Bristol entertains more than 40,000 per year and has been in business for more than 17 years. It locates itself in the United Coal Company's Humanities Center, a theater boasting a modern 756 seat auditorium.

The Bristol Ballet Company dates back to 1959 and enjoys an excellent reputation throughout the nation.

In addition to this, Bristol boasts a concert choir and its own art museum.

Education

Virginia Intermont College is a four year liberal arts co-ed institution.

King College is a small co-ed liberal arts school located in East Bristol.

Virginia Highlands Community College is located in Abingdon.

Bristol College is situated on the Tennessee side.

East Tennessee State University is a large institution located in nearby Johnson City, Tennessee.

History

It all started here with the Cherokees. Legend refers to the land around here as "Big Meet Camp" because the deer and buffalo liked the local environment. In the middle of the 18th Century, the Scotch-Irish settled here. We are told that these locals played a very important part in the outcome of the Revolutionary War when some 900 took part in the Battle of Kings Mountain in South Carolina —very crucial to the War's outcome.

The first country music recording was done by Victor her in 1927.

The visitor to Bristol is always intrigued by the fact that the main street, now known as State Street, serves as the boundary line between Virginia and Tennessee. This provides the region with twin cities that appear to work together in a spirit of fellowship and cooperation. One should not infer from this phenomenon that this business of two states in one community has been without its problems. The contrast in tax laws between the states has resulted in businesses and industries basing themselves on the side of the state line that is most favorable to their individual needs.

Over the years criminals and misdemeanants have played tag with officials from the two jurisdictions by hopscotching over the State Street boundary. Witness the local hospital that was constructed with funds from both sides of the street. The hospital is in two states with the delivery room on the "Volunteer" state side of the building. All of it makes for a very intriguing place to visit.

Geography

As we said earlier, Bristol is divided between two states. In addition to that is the fact that within 55 miles of the city five states come together; namely, Virginia, Tennessee, Kentucky, West Virginia, and North Carolina. Bristol along with Johnson City and Kingsport —both in Tenneessee, make up what is known as the "tri-cities."

Rolling hills and mountains form the picturesque backdrop for this area. Like so much of the state there is much to fill the lens of your camera. Weather is moderate and changes to four regular seasons.

Population for Bristol, Virginia, is about 19,000 while for its sister city on the Tennessee side it runs about 25,000.

Transportation & Logistics

The nearby Tri-Cities Airport is served primarily by Piedmont Airlines. Greyhound, Trailways, and Bristol-Jenkins are the bus companies going over the highways. The Norfolk & Southern Railroad handles the trackside transport.

The motorist will find that nearby I-81 goes west to Knoxville 118 miles away. In the opposite direction is Roanoke some 143 miles distant. The interstate highway system finds I-77 and I-40 within 75 miles of I-81. From a transportation standpoint, one could ask for nothing more accessible than Bristol.

GALAX

Lodgings: (703)
Midtowner Motel, 303 N. Main St., 236-5127
Rose Lane Motel, 312 W. Stuart Dr., 236-5177
Hills Motel, I-77, 728-7664
Knob Hill Motor Lodge, 305 E. Stuart Dr., 728-2131
The Stable, US 52S, 728-7623
Towne House Motel, US 58 & 221E, 728-7027
Osborne Motel, Independence, 773-3221
Cascade Mountain Inn, Fancy Gap, 728-2300
Doe Run Lodge, Fancy Gap, 398-2212
Lake View Motel & Restaurant, Fancy Gap, 728-7841
Mountain Top Motel, Fancy Gap, 728-9414

Campgrounds: (703)
R J Ranch & Campground, 766-3703
Fox Trail Inn Campground, 728-7776

Dining: (703)
D's Doughnut Shoppe & Restaurant, S. Main St., 236-4455
Kentucky Fried Chicken, 526 E. Stuart Dr., 236-2261
Steer House Restaurant, 1101 E. Stuart Dr., 236-4111
Winchester's Restaurant, 303 N. Main St., 236-5127
Corner Restaurant, Hillsville, 728-9295
Druther's Restaurant, I-77, 728-4213
Jerry's Restaurant, Highway 221, 728-2202
R-J Ranch Pelican Pier Seafood Restaurant, Hillsville, 766-3703
The Shenandoah, Hickory Hill Shopping Center, 728-3251
Ogle's Sandwich Shoppe, 121 Independence Ave., 773-3662
The Quick Chek & Paul's Restaurant, Main St., 773-3451
Doe Run Lodge, Fancy Gap, 398-2212
Lake View Restaurant, Fancy Gap, 728-7841
Mountain Top Restaurant, Fancy Gap, 728-9196
Blairtown Drive-In, Church St., 744-2402
Fries Food Store & Luncheonette, Main St., 744-7721

GALAX-CARROLL COUNTY-GRAYSON COUNTY

Potpourri

Population: Galax - 6500; Carroll County - 27,300; Grayson County - 16,300. Elevation: Galax - 2500 to 3400 feet; Carroll County - 1162 to 3600 feet; Grayson County 2300 to 5729 feet.

The area enjoys four seasons with about 47 inches of rain and several snowfalls that will average about 15-20 inches per year.

Galax is about 90 miles from Roanoke and approximately 70 miles from Winston-Salem, N.C. Principal highways serving the community are US 58 and 221 as well as I-77. This latter Interstate road ties Galax into I-81 and US 52. Commercial air service is provided from Roanoke and Winston-Salem. Rail service is furnished by the Norfolk & Southern Railroad while bus is provided by both Greyhound and Trailways.

Galax was named after the galax leaf which grows around the Blue Ridge Parkway near Galax. These leaves are used extensively by florists, the country over, in the making up of dried arrangements. As can be imagined this plant plays an important role in the local economy. Approximately 19,000 people are employed by the area's principal manufacturing industries. Industry is fairly well diversified and includes furniture, textile, apparel, lumber products in its number.

Old Fiddlers Convention, Galax

Events & Places

OLD TIME FIDDLER'S CONVENTION — Annually on the second weekend of August is this world renowned event which includes string music, folk songs, and dancing. This is where lovers of country and mountain music assemble from near and far. This annual competition is sponsored by the local Moose Lodge.

THE JEFF MATTHEWS MEMORIAL MUSEUM — 606 W. Stuart Drive, Galax. You may view two authentically restored cabins as well as artifacts, maps, magazines, 16 cases of knives — all depicting the life and time of this locale over the years. A fringe benefit for the visitor is the display of big game trophies contributed to the museum by individuals from their hunts in far flung places. Closed on Monday and Tuesday.

CRAFTS — 206 N. Main Street — The local community action agency and native craftsmen cooperate to bring the public the nation's widest variety of authentic hand made crafts. The public is invited to browse or buy.

GRUNDY

Lodgings: (703)
Anchor Inn, E. Grundy
Gateway to the Breaks, Breaks Interstate
Justice Motel, Tookland
Short Ridge Motel, Van Sant
Van Sant Motel, Van Sant

Dining: (703)
Western Sizzlin', W. Grundy
Hardee's, W. Grundy
Druthers Resaurant, US 460
Wanda's Steak House, US 460

BUCHANAN COUNTY & GRUNDY

We doubt that there are very many guidebooks in print that have included this region of Virginia. In light of the fact that it is less populous and slightly "off the beaten path" it is not as well known as other parts of the state. Hopefully, this will serve as an introductory to the region for many prospective tourists. We believe that this will give you an interesting insight into a region that has been ignored by outsiders over the years.

One reaches this area by taking US 460 from Tazewell. In the opposite direction one would use US 19 until it intersects with US 460. Buchanan County is bordered on one side by West Virginia and on another side by Kentucky. One might note that the state itself forms a neck in the southwest and to the south it borders on Tennessee and North Carolina. Before leaving the subject of routings we should mention that a cutoff exists at Narrows on Va. 61. We are reluctant to offer highway suggestions because they are as diversified as the points of origination from within the state. Make good use of your state road map.

Buchanan County was formed in 1858 and was named after President James Buchanan who was then in office. It was first explored in 1750 but very few settlers came until after the Revolution. However, it was not until the 1930's that there was any appreciable settlement. It was the advent of the coal mining industry that brought newcomers to the area. Grundy, the county seat, is the county's only incorporated town. Its population is about 2400 while the county has about 37,000.

Located in the Appalachian Plateau the county is uniformly mountainous with numerous streams separated by sharp ridges. On the Kentucky line the elevation is about 885 feet to 3375 feet. Big A Mountain on Sandy Ridge adjacent to Russell County, Virginia, is the principal landmark of the county.

Humidity is pleasing here. The area has four separate seasons with a bit more precipitation than less mountainous parts of the state. Precipitation here is reported at about 47 inches per year.

Prior to the advent of mining to the region lumbering was ranked as the leading industry. However, lumber has taken a back seat to coal mining. We learn that the labor force within the county involved in coal production is over 8000. Buchanan County ranks number one in the state for coal production. All four types of coal production are done in the county, namely: deep, strip, truck, and auger. Needless to say railroads are vital to this region. Exportation of coal has been so important to the history of the Norfolk & Western Railroad. The railroad has ably capitalized on the shipping of this commodity to such an extent that it has traditionally been one of the most financially successful transportation companies in the United States. It is today known as the Norfolk & Southern.

There is a local airport providing service for smaller aircraft. Commercial air service can be secured from Bluefield, W. Va., some 55 miles distant or from the Tri-City Airport in Tennessee some 105 miles away.

MOUNTAIN MISSION SCHOOL — Established in 1921 this home for orphaned children numbers some 300 ranging from one year to 21. This coeducational institution attempts to take over the total education of unfortunate children that are either orphaned or find that their families can not bring them up. They are given a Christian education with as many of the amenities as the budget permits. The school offers room, board, a program of athletics, as well as the other offerings found in a boarding school situation. Children of all races and creeds are taken into the school. Most of the children come from Mountain family backgrounds. Further Information: Mountain Mission School, P.O. Box 1440, Grundy, VA 24614; 703/935-2954.

BREAKS INTERSTATE PARK — KENTUCKY/VIRGINIA
The park is located seven miles from Elkhorn City, Kentucky and eight miles from Haysi, Virginia on KY-VA 80. From Grundy you take US 460 for a few miles to VA 609. This park was created in 1954 by joint action of the legislatures of the states of Kentucky and Virginia encompassing 4500 acres of green woodlands and skyscraping mountain scenery.

Visitors to the park will find that this region is steeped in folklore. There are tales about hidden silver fortunes, the Hatfield-McCoy Feud, the Shawnee Pow Wow Cave and Daniel Boone. Here there is a beautiful blending of fact, fiction, and fable. It is for you to determine which is which.

Arriving at the park the visitor is greeted by the modern Visitor's Center which is the focal point of a complex that contains exhibits and displays of the natural and historical features of the area. The exhibit on coal is one of the more popular ones. There is an amphitheater in a natural shaded setting where educational as well as entertainment programs are held. This is the site for the Annual Gospel Song Festival.

The facilities here number a well appointed motor lodge open between April and October. There are 34 units. There are also some two bedroom fully equipped family cottages that are open the year round. From April thru October there are spaces for campers in a select wooded area. There are picnic shelters for groups as well as picnic areas with tables and grills scattered throughout the park. Diners are treated to a spectacular view from the very delightful restaurant at Rhododendron Lodge on the Canyon Rim. You will be happy to learn that there is also a gift shop at the lodge. Swimmers can use the beautiful olympic sized swimming pool with its accompanying bath house.

It is here at this park that the Russell River has carved the largest canyon east of the Mississippi. This virgin canyon is 1600 feet deep and more than five miles long. This beautiful canyon winds around an imposing pyramid of rocks known as the Towers. It is over a half mile long and 1/3 mile wide. This natural wonder is often called the "Grand Canyon of the South." Breaks Canyon is estimated to be 250 million years old of the late Paleozoic era.

Laurel Lake is a natural blending of very green woodlands and very clear blue mountain water. The lake is well stocked with bass and bluegill. Pedal boats are available for rental.

Quoting from the folder put out by the park people is a section that we quote verbatim: "Tips to Visitors-Wear comfortable clothes and bring your camera and binoculars for hiking and exploring. Detailed park and trail maps are available at the Park office or Visitors' Center." Need we say more!

Park Information and Cottage Reservations: Breaks Interstate Park, Breaks, VA 24607; 703/865-4413. Motel Reservations: Breaks Motor Lodge, Breaks, VA 24607; 703/865-4414.

For general information on Buchanan County and Grundy contact: Buchanan County Chamber of Commerce, P.O. Box 672, Grundy, VA 24614; 703/935-4147.

— *Virginia State Travel Service*

Largest Canyon East of the Mississippi, In Breaks Interstate Park on the Virginia-Kentucky Border

LEE COUNTY

Lodgings: (703)
Lee-Shelburne Motel, US 58/421, Pennington Gap
Pennington Gap Motel, US 58/421, Pennington Gap
Cumberland Park Motel, Ewing
Jonesville Motor Lodge, US 58, Jonesville

Dining
Cumberland Bowl Town House, US 58, Jonesville
Country Hearth, US 58, Jonesville
Driftwood Drive-In & Restaurant, US 421, Pennington Gap
Patio Drive-In, US 58, Pennington Gap
Town & Country Restaurant, Pennington Gap
Sunny Acres Restaurant, VA 622

Potpourri
Located in the extreme southwest tip of the Commonwealth of Virginia this county of some 26,000 persons is flanked by Kentucky and Tennessee. This is an area virtually untouched by the industrial complex. It is an area steeped with scenic beauty in an environment of rugged mountains. Here is a place to explore for its natural characteristics. This is where you come when you want to get away from the cares of the world. This is an opportunity to make your own prescription for an unfettered way of life.

What To See And Do

CUMBERLAND GAP NATIONAL HISTORICAL PARK — If the Commonwealth of Virginia has a point — then you will go through it to enter the Park. But, what is even more to the "point" is the fact that you will be retracing Colonial history. For, it was back in 1750 that a Dr. Thomas Walker and party left from Albemarle County (Thomas Jefferson Country) in search of some very rich grazing lands which were reported to abound with buffalo, deer, and all manner of game. The Cherokees could make the trip on foot from their native North Carolina. They could even take on other tribes. But, it was not for Dr. Walker and his party to do. They failed on their quest. However, he did find his gateway to the great west and he named it "Cave Gap."

It was because of Walker that the way was paved to the lands beyond the Mississippi. Daniel Boone's courage some few years later expanded on the "gateway" and undoubtedly resulted in the formation of the Commonwealth of Kentucky that today exists.

The park in three states: Kentucky, Tennessee, and Virginia preserves the pathways of the early pioneers on their move to the great west. Camping, hiking, nature trails, museums, and beautiful scenery is your reward. Contact: Superintendent, Cumberland Gap National Historical Park, P.O. Box 840, Middlesboro, KY 40965; 606/248-2817.

CAVE SPRINGS — Located at Dryden on VA 621. This is a recreation area with camping and picnic facilities with some beautiful scenery.

SAND CAVE — This is one of nature's wonders located high above sea level atop Cumberland Mountain. Near Ewing.

NATURAL BRIDGE — A natural rock formation which serves as a bridge on VA 622.

LAKE KEOKEE — Nestled in the mountains with opportunities for camping, fishing, hiking, and other outdoor activities.

POWELL MOUNTAIN — Beautiful vista is to be seen from the top.

CUDJO'S CAVERNS — Said to be the fourth largest caverns in the world.

HENSLEY'S SETTLEMENT — A small isolated community atop Brush Mountain is the historic village of the Hensley Family. The restored community is open to the public year round.

For more information on this very picturesque area contact: Chamber of Commerce, 105 E. Morgan Ave., Pennington Gap, VA 24277.

MARION
Lodgings: (703)
Holiday Inn, 1600 Main St., US 11 & I-81, 783-3193
Quality Inn, Virginia House, I-81, Exit 17, 783-5112
Lorenzen's Motel, 606 S. Main St., 783-2316
Marion Motel, 435 S. Main St., 783-8511
Mt. Rogers Inn, I-81, Exit 13, Chilhowie, 646-8981
Rainbow Autel, US 11E, Chilhowie, 646-8411
Salina Motel, Main St., Saltville, 496-4444
Village Motel, I-81, Exit 18, Atkins, 783-5811

Campgrounds
Hungry Mother Campgrounds, Inc., 783-2406
Hungry Mother State Park, 783-3422
Mt. Rogers National Recreation Area, 783-5196
Tumbling Creak, Saltville

Dining
Bassett's, Marion Plaza, 783-8866
Beacon, 230 E. Main St., 783-2122
City Drug Store, Main St., 783-7133
Cumbow's, I-81, Ex. 18, Groseclose, 686-4759
Happy's Pizza, 437 N. Main St., 783-5515
Hardee's, 347 N. Main, 783-6441
Hilda's Luncheonette, Main St. (Marion Drug), 783-7241
Holiday Inn, US 11E, 783-3193
Hungry Mother Grill, Va. 16N, State Park, 783-7300
Jaron Steak House, US 11, Chilhowie, 646-5331
Kentucky Fried Chicken, 790 N. Main St., 783-4919
K-Mart, Marion Plaza, 783-5153
Marion Diner, Va. 16S, 783-4918
McDonald's, 1104 N. Main St., 783-5871
Mt. Rogers Inn, I-81, Exit 13, 646-8981
Piggly Wiggly, Parkway Plaza, 783-7215
Pioneer, US 11E, 783-4994
Pizza Hut, 1038 N. Main St., 783-8081
Rainbow Restaurant, US 11E, Chilhowie, 646-8411
Ray's Kingsburger, Brunswick Lane, 783-8441
Rose's Store, Parkway Plaza, 783-3101
Royal Oak, US 11E, 783-5771
Salina Restaurant, Main St., Saltville, 496-4444
Steak House, Va. 16S, 783-8730
Taco Hut, 534 S. Main St., 783-5000
Tastee Freeze, Chilhowie, 646-3119
The Salt Shaker, Ball Park Ave., Saltville, 496-4261
Troutdale Dining Room, Va. 16S, Troutdale, 677-3671
Village Restaurant, I-81, Exit 18, Atkins, 783-5811

MARION & SMYTH COUNTY

Smyth County was formed from seven other counties in the year 1832. Its new county seat was named in honor of the famed Revolutionary War hero, the "Swamp Fox," General Francis Marion. We are told that the Indians of 12,000 years into the past adopted the buffalo trails for their own use. (One of them is the Wilderness Trail). US 11 and I-81 closely parallel these early trails. It was through these trails that the only usable route to Kentucky and the western frontier was traversed by the pioneers.

Smyth County's story dates back as far as 10,000 B.C. Based on spear point findings dating back to the Stone Age we now have evidence of Paleo-Indians who were the nomadic hunters of that day. Fossilized deposits in the salt ponds of Saltville revealed a mastadon bone with an embedded spear point.

Smyth County has been a treasure trove for archaeologists for many years. There are many traces of various types of Indians from 8000 B.C. to around 1700 A.D. This is rich land and has proven fruitful to Indians over the many years as a proverbial happy hunting ground. There is record of campsites near water and cultivated fields. It was Saltville where the ponds were a source of much of the salt that was sought by both the animals and the Indians, themselves.

This region was well known and vital to the development of the Virginia colony in the pre-Revolution era. In 1750, the outpost western habitation was in what is today Smith County. The region was known to be inhabited by both Cherokees and Shawnees. These tribes had an impact on the lives of the Colonists of the area.

Major combat actions took place within the county during the Civil War. They were attributed to the presence of the salt works in Saltville. It is said that the output of salt during the war was 10,000 bushels per day over a sustained period of six months.

This is an area rich in history. It begins with prehistoric times and evolves to the modern recorded period of the Colonies and the westward march of the pioneers. The story traverses the period of civil war and comes to the tranquility that we enjoy here today. It is a beautiful region wealthy in appearance as well as in the hardy stock that today lives on her soil.

Potpourri

Elevation in the county ranges from 1740 feet to 5729 while in Marion it is 2300 feet. Population for Smyth County is about 33,500 with the Town of Marion having slightly over 7000. Rainfall averages 46 inches with approximately 20 inches snowfall.

LOGISTICS AND LOCATION — The region is served by I-81, I-77, US 11, and Va. 16. In addition to the Mountain Empire Airport for general aircraft 10 miles east of Marion, there are commercial facilities at Tri-Cities Airport 60 miles to the southwest via I-81. Rail service is provided by the Norfolk & Southern with bus service by Greyhound.

Education
EMORY & HENRY COLLEGE — Founded in 1836, Emory & Henry College is a four-year, coeducational, liberal arts college. The College is affiliated with The United Methodist Church and is accredited by the Southern Assoication. The College was named for John Emory, a dynamic young Methodist bishop of the 1800's, and Patrick Henry, the famous Virginia orator of the Revolutionary War.

Currently Emory & Henry enrolls about 800 students, almost equally divided between males and females. The academic program includes primary fields of study in traditional liberal arts programs such as art, biology, history, music, and political science, along with pre-professional training in areas such as medical technology, mass communications, and business.

The entire campus of Emory & Henry has been designated as a Virginia Historic Landmark, primarily because of the College's role in pioneering higher education in the region. Visitors to the campus will enjoy a number of historic and architecturally distinctive buildings such as Waterhouse-Carriger Hall, Byars Hall, and the Tobias Smyth House.

To reach Emory & Henry, take exit 10 off Interstate-81 and follow signs to the campus.

For more information, write or call: Public Relations Office, Emory & Henry College, Emory, VA 24327, 703/944-3121.

Things To Do
THE CLINCH MOUNTAIN WILDLIFE MANAGEMENT AREA — Located northwest of Saltville is the state's first fee fishing program which begun in 1968. Fishermen can pay a daily fee for which they can go after the trout in the 300 acre mountaintop lake or in Big Tumbling Creek. From a folder on the area we use these words to described the creek, "Big Tumbling is one of the most beautiful streams in the country. Its sparkling waters thunder down the mountain through deep gorges and into deep, cold ponds where trout love to hide." (Editor's Note: This copy was written on a day in which the temperature outside exceeded 94 degrees).

MOUNT ROGERS NATIONAL RECREATION AREA — A large portion of the county is within the boundaries of this area. It is a 154,000 acre section of the Jefferson National Forest. It is named after the highest peak in the state, Mount Rogers (5729 feet).

There are more than 75 trout streams as well as several warm water lakes. Fishing is reported as excellent. The area contains five well equipped campgrounds. There is opportunity for picnics, swimming, hiking, and horeseback riding. There are more than 300 miles of trails which include 115 miles that are dedicated to foot and ski travel. Fifty-eight miles of the Appalachian Trail run through the area. National Recreation Area Headquarters are located on US 16 just south of Marion.

We suggest that you secure a most informative folder entitled, "Recreation Areas Mount Rogers NRA Virginia." This excellent piece contains a line map of the area as well as a detailed description of the various recreation areas of the park. The folder also includes details as to facilities for the various recreation areas. For further information contact: Mount Rogers National Recreation Area, Route 1, Box 303, Marion, VA 24354, 703/783-5196.

HUNGRY MOTHER STATE PARK — This 2180 acre park is visited by more than 300,000 people per year. It is located on US 16 three miles north of Marion. Fishing, swimming, and boating can be enjoyed on the 108 acre lake. Visitors can enjoy the beach as well. Hiking and horseback riding on the park's 16 miles of trails offer more alternatives for park enjoyment. The park includes a Visitors Center containing exhibits of wildlife and plants to be found in the area. This park includes cabin rentals as well as campsites with access to modern restroom and shower facilities. For further information: Hungry Mother State Park, Route 5, Box 109, Marion, VA 24354, 703/783-3422.

HUNGRY MOTHER ARTS & CRAFTS FESTIVAL — This annual three day event draws people from many miles around. In addition to the many crafts represented, there is regional musical and dancing entertainment. Further information concerning dates can be secured from: The Smyth County Chamber of Commerce, 200 Main Street, Marion, VA 24354, 703/783-3161.

PULASKI

Lodgings: (703)
Dogwood Lodge, US 11W, Radford; 639-9338
Executive Motel, US 11W, Radford, 639-1664
Red Carpet Inn, I-81, Exit 31, 980-2230
Ranch House Motel, US 11 & Va. 100, Dublin, 674-4611

Dining: (703)
Rib & Sirloin Restaurant, I-81, Exit 31, 980-2230
Ranch House Restaurant, I-81, Exit 32, Dublin, 674-9223

Potpourri

Both the town and county take their name from Count Casimir Pulaski, exiled Polish patriot that fought on the side of the colonists during the Revolutionary War. The town has a population of approximately 10,100. Total for the county is about 35,300. This very beautiful rural area has rolling hills and mountains. The county contains a portion of the Jefferson National Forest as well as the Claytor Lake State Park. Elevation in certain parts of the county is approximately 2500 feet.

This is an agriculturally oriented area that has diversified industry throughout the county. The industrial line up is composed of textiles, furniture, clothing, and lumber.

Motorists have a choice of such highways as I-81, US 11, and Va. 100. The closest commercial air transportation is available at Roanoke. New River Valley Airport, located in nearby Dublin, accommodates smaller aircraft.

NEW RIVER COMMUNITY COLLEGE — This two year school is part of the Virginia Community College System and is located at Dublin. Nearby four year colleges are located at Radford and Blacksburg; Radford University and Virginia Tech respectively.

NEWBERN — This historic town of the county was issued a land grant by King Geroge III in 1772 but it was not until 1810 that a town was planned. Located in Newbern is the "old jail" which was in use between 1839 and 1893. It has been designated as a Historic Landmark. The building, today, houses Newbern's temporary museum and is opened on a limited basis by appointment. For further details the principals can be reached by calling: 703/674-5888 or 674-5853. This quaint old village is located on the Wilderness Trail. Newbern is also the home for Ruritan National, America's only rural civic club. It has a national membership of approximately 40,000 members.

CLAYTOR LAKE — The first known development here took place prior to 1745. The region was settled by Dunkards and was fittingly known as Dunkards Bottom. This was the home of Col. William Christian, chairman of the committee to draw up the Fincastle Resolutions. They preceded the Declaration of Independence by about 18 months. Many battles were fought in this region during the early history of the nation.

Claytor Lake stretches 21 miles along the New River in Pulaski County and was created by the Appalachian Power Company in 1939 at the time they built Claytor Dam. The shoreline is more than 100 miles and the lake covers in excess of 4500 acres.

The Claytor Lake State Park is just short of 500 acres including camping, cottages, and beach. This is one of the few state parks that allows motorboating. Available for rental are 12 cottages, 170 tent camping spots, and 97 trailer spaces.

Other facilities include hiking and riding trails. There is a modern bathhouse adjacent to a sand beach. The state also operates a modern marina. The park headquarters houses a museum containing relics of this area. Further information may be secured by writing: Claytor Lake State Park, Dublin, VA 24084.

For general information on Pulaski County contact: Pulaski County Chamber of Commerce, P.O. Box 169, Pulaski, VA 24301, 703/980-1991.

Special Events
Visitors to the Pulaski area will be interested in checking their calendars during their visitation. The annual Pulaski County Flea Market and Antique Show is held annually during the first weekend of June at the New River Valley Fair Grounds. Further information can be secured from the sponsoring Lions Club.

FIDDLER'S CONVENTION — This is held in mid July at the same fair gounds and is sponsored by the Odd Fellows.

During the end of July there is generally a quilt show sponsored by the Cheerful Lady's Club.

Also, watch for the New River Valley Horse Show during the early part of August.

PULASKI COUNTY FAIR — This is held annually during the second week of August. Contact: New River Valley Recreation, Inc., Rt. 1, Box 152-A, Dublin, VA 24084, 703/674-5115.

Virginia Mountain Crafts Guild Fair, Claytor Lake State Park is held on Labor Day Weekend.

Flea Market & Antique Show held annually third weekend of September and sponsored by Dublin Lions Club.

Fall Festival/Harvest Bazaar held at Newbern. You may contact the Historical Society there.

COUNT PULASKI CELEBRATION — Annually on the third Saturday of October. This is sponsored by the Celebration Committee.

For specific dates on all of these you may either contact the references given above or the Pulaski Chamber of Commerce.

TAZEWELL

Lodgings: (703)
John's Motel, Rt. 19 & US 460, 988-5521
Tazewell Motel, US 19/460W, 988-5531
Fincastle Motor Inn, Fincastle Tpke, 988-2531
Hill Top Motel, Doran, 964-2551
Justus Motel, Tookland, 935-4868
Shortridge Motel, Vansant, 935-2968

Dining: (703)
Brass Ring, Deel, 935-4433
Brent's Burger Bar, Keen Mt., 498-4020
Burger Barn, Breaks Maxie, 531-8813
Burger Queen, US 460, E. Front, Richlands, 964-4947
Coleman's Family Restaurant, 105 Norfolk Ave., Richlands, 963-2775
Cuz's Uptown Barbecue, Pounding Mill, Richlands, 964-9014
Dairy Queen, 817 Fincastle, Tazewell, 988-4181
Dial Rock Restaurant, Blue-Taze Rd., Tazewell, 988-7726
Dotson's Drive Inn, Grundy, 935-7880
John's Restaurant, Rt. 19 & US 460, 988-5521
Druthers Restaurant, Vansant, 935-8711
Frenche's Bakery, Anchorage Shpg. Ctr., Grundy, 935-8703
Fuller's Dairy Bar, Whitewood, 259-7070
Giovanni's Pizza, Magic City Shpg. Ctr., Richlands, 963-0166
Giovanni's Pizza Garden, Oakwood, 498-7042
Italian Villa, Inc., Richlands Mall, Richlands, 963-2594
Johnson's Drive In Restaurant, Adria, Tazewell, 988-2000
Kentucky Fried Chicken, Royal City, 935-8642
    Doran, 964-9232
Hardee's, 900 E. Fincastle, Tazewell, 988-9500
    Grundy, 935-8255
    2020 2nd, Richlands, 963-0150
King Kone, W. Front, Richlands, 963-7875
Long John Silver's, Grundy, 935-7300
    901 Fincastle Rd., Tazewell, 988-9043
    US 460, Richlands, 964-2660
Louie's Restaurant, Fincastle Tpke, Tazewell, 988-7108
M & M Restaurant, Doran, 964-6945
Mabel's Country Kitchen, Cedar Bluff, 964-9333
McDonald's, 599 Market St., Tazewell, 988-9747
    2970 Clinch, Richlands, 963-9866
Maggie's Drive In, Slate Creek, Dwight, 259-7327
McLendy's, Grundy, 935-8594
    Cedar Bluff Rd., Cedar Bluff, 963-0919
Mullins Motel & Restaurant, Claypool Hill, 964-4057
Musick's Restaurant, Slate Creek, 935-8390

Pizza Hut, Doran, Richlands, 963-0515
  Grundy, 935-4539
  645 E. Riverside Dr., Tazewell, 988-5556
  107 E. Front, 964-9635
Rainbow Drive Inn, Vansant, 935-2796
Ramey Dairy Bar, Vansant, 935-7270
Dairy Queen, 1251 Front, Richlands, 963-0249
Starlins Country Cooking, Deskins, 597-8914
Tastee Freez, Doran, 964-2418
  Oakwood, 498-4154
V & V Restaurant, US 460, Richlands, 964-2182
Wanda's Restaurant, Tookland, 935-6111
Western Sizzlin' Steak House, Grundy, 935-7111
Boggie's Restaurant & Lounge, E. Fincastle, Tazewell, 988-7858
Western Steer Family Steak House, Richlands Mall, Richlands, 964-6917
  Cumberland Park, Tazewell, 988-9502
Western World Family Steak House, Claypool Hill Mall, Richlands, 963-2744
Yuvone Dairy Hut, Grundy, 935-4427
Cocozza's Deli, Main St., 988-9628
Coal Bucket Deli, Tazewell Mall, Tazewell, 988-9100

Potpourri

Tazewell County is in the southwest part of Virginia. Average elevation here is 2381 feet. There are four seasons of the year with average rainfall of about 42 inches and snowfall of about 34 inches.

The area is served by US 19, US 460, and US 52. There is accessibility to I-77 and I-81. People coming to the county have a choice of air service from either the Tri-Cities Airport in Blountville, TN, or the airport at Bluefield. Richlands has an airport for chartered equipment. Trailways operates the inter-city bus service while the Norfolk & Southern provides rail service.

Southwest Community College serves the needs for approximately 5000 students. The school is located about 20 miles south of the Town of Tazewell and is part of the state community college system. In nearby Bluefield, West Virginia, are Bluefield State College, West Virginia Business College and McLain's Business College as well as Executive Secretarial Business College. Radford University and Virginia Tech are within 2½ hours.

County population is estimated at 45,000. The Town of Tazewell is almost 5000. Town of Bluefield is at 5500 whereas the combined Bluefield, Virginia and Bluefield, West Virginia, is estimated at 30,000. The Town of Richland is about 6000.

The area's economy is based on a combination of mining, agriculture, and manufacturing. Coal has been the leading contributor to the mineral wealth with limestone ranked number two. Coal deposits were first noted as early as 1750 but the first production did not take place until 1882 when a mine near Pocahontas was opened. There are 36 mines of four different categories within the county. They break down as follows: 3-triple, 9-strip, 21-truck, and 3-auger.

The history of this region has always been associated with hard work. This held true in prehistoric times as well as within the range of recorded history. The Indians competed for the use of the hunting grounds and it culminated in a two day battle at Rich Mountain in 1786. The Cherokees were the winners. This resulted in making the area safe for the subsequent development which was to come to the area. The only examples of Indian picture writing in southwest Virginia are to be found at Handkerchief Rock as well as Paint Lick Mountain.

For the security of the region it was mandatory that consideration be given to the security of the pioneers. In the year 1772 old Fort Whitten was built by the first permanent white settlers. It was built by Thomas Whitten and his neighbors to protect themselves against attack by the Indians. During the next few years other fortifications were to be built by others.

It is to be noted that Richlands was an early site for hunting explorations and by 1782 a militia station was to be located there. It was one of America's most western outposts.

This area was adjacent to the part of Virginia that broke away and was to become the new state of West Virginia. Loyalties were markedly in support of the Confederate cause. In other pages we alluded to the heroism of Molly Tynes who took a wild 44 mile horseback ride to warn that "The Yankees are coming at dawn." This heroic action resulted in the defeat of the Union forces.

HISTORIC CRAB ORCHARD MUSEUM & PIONEER PARK
Located in Tazewell on US 19/460 on a complex of 110 acres. It has been designated as a prehistoric and historic archaeological landmark and is also listed in the National Register of Historic Places. The history of the county and southwest Virginia is depicted here from prehistoric to present times. The visitor to the museum will find representative artifacts as well as other items of interest. There is a crafts shop on the premises. Information concerning the times that the museum is opened may be obtained by contacting: P.O. Box 12, Tazewell, VA 24651, 703/988-6755.

WISE COUNTY
Lodgings: (703)
Austin Motel, US 23, Pound, 796-5449
Carriage Hill Motel, US 23N, Wise, 328-8071
Country Boy Motel, US 23, Big Stone Gap, 523-0374
Deluxe Motel, Indian Creek, Pound, 796-5416
Jefferson Motel, 540 Park Ave., Norton, 679-1280
Mountaineer Motel, E. Park Ave. NE, Norton, 679-0094
Old Virginia Motel, US 23, Pound, 796-5421
Park Motel, 937 Park Ave. NE, Norton, 679-2550
Ramada Inn, US 58, Duffield, 431-4300
Three-Way Motel, Main St., Coeburn, 395-3311
Trail Motel, US 23 & 58, Big Stone Gap, 523-1171
Travelers Motel, US 23, Pound, 796-5428
Western Hills, US 58, Coeburn, 395-3371
The Inn at Wise Courthouse, Main St., Wise, 328-2241

Dining:
Pizza Inn, 1650 Park Ave., Norton, 679-0664
Western Steer Family Steakhouse, 1728 Park Ave. NW, Norton, 679-0673
The Ice Cream Parlor, Norton
Burger Queen, Norton, 679-4854
Berry's Dining Room, 1009 Park Ave., Norton, 679-2075
Brass Lantern Restaurant, Norton
The Inn at Wise Courthouse, Main St., Wise, 328-2241
Mountain Top Deli, Coeburn Rd., Wise, 328-2837
Foxie's Three Way Chili, Big Stone Gap, 523-2069

WISE COUNTY
Just about the most southwestern county in the state, Wise County is bordered by the State of Kentucky on the west. Not too far to the northeast is the State of West Virginia. Distance from metropolitan Tri-City, Tennessee area is 52 miles to the southeast. Population for the county is approximately 44,000. County seat is Wise with about 4000 residents. The largest town in the county is Big Stone Gap with approximately 4800. Other towns in the county are Coeburn with 2600; Appalachia with 2400; Pound with 1100 and Saint Paul with 1150.

Norton
The City of Norton, contiguous to Wise County, has a population of approximately 4800.

Education
The area is served by CLINCH VALLEY COLLEGE with an enrollment of about 1150. This is a four year university college of the University of Virginia. Degrees are offered in 14 fields; the newest being in Mining Management. The college is located at Wise.

MOUNTAIN EMPIRE COMMUNITY COLLEGE — This two year college is a part of the Virginia Community College System and is located two miles southeast of Big Stone Gap. Enrollment here is about 2700.

History

Needless to say, the Indians were the first ones here. Both the Cherokees and Shawnees actively competed for the privilege of using this very wealthy hunting ground. The region was plentiful with buffalo, elk, bear, deer, turkey and wild geese.

The area was not settled until 1800 and moved at a very slow pace. It was some 50 years before, that Captain George Grist, a scout for George Washington, explored the region. It is stated that he returned from exploration with a piece of coal.

From the outset this was a very difficult region for settlers. Travel was severely handicapped by the difficult terrain. From the standpoint of cultivation there was very little in the way of adequate farmland.

Daniel Boone knew the area well as he led frequent scouting parties as well as groups of settlers. Buried in Powell Valley is his son, James, murdered by the Cherokees.

Wise County was formed in 1856 and started with 250 people in the town that was to become Wise. The county was named for Henry Alexander Wise who was Governor of Virginia at the time. The area was very heavily hit by the Civil War with considerable loss of property and lives. There were several bloody battles fought at Pound Gap.

It was during the year 1880 that tracts of land commenced being purchased by coal operators. The boom came in 1890 with the pending arrival of the railroads. It was during the period following the end of World War II that the dieselization of railroads and the strength of imported oil greatly affected the local economy. It was during the 1960's that strip mining began to play an integral part in the local economy. In the 70's the energy crisis had an impact and today we find that soft coal is the key to a healthy local situation. County residents are optimistic about their economic prospects for the coming years as the result of the return of coal to the national energy scene.

Potpourri

Sharp ridges and narrow valleys and varying elevation ranging from 1400 feet to as high as 4162 feet. There are four seasons with an annual precipitation of about 46 inches. Humidity here is pleasing and temperatures remain moderate for the season.

There is ample railroad service to handle the exportation of the locally produced coal. Motorists will find US 23 and US 58 as the principal highways serving the county. Smaller aircraft utilize the Lonesome Pine Airport. Commercial air service is available from the Tri-City, Tennessee Airport some 40 miles distant from Norton.

What To See And What To Do
Big Stone Gap

JOHN FOX, JR. HOUSE — Located at 117 Shawnee Avenue is the home of the famed 19th Century novelist. Open to the public from the end of June to Labor Day. Contact: John Fox, Jr. House, 106 E. Gilly Ave., Big Stone Gap, VA 24219.

JUNE TOLLIVER HOUSE — Here, you can turn back the clock to the 19th Century as well as patronize the gift shop with its inventory of mountain-made crafts.

SOUTHWEST VIRGINIA MUSEUM — Open to the public daily excepting Monday. There is no admission charge at this state operated museum which is housed in a former residence dating back to the 1880's. Exhibits include cultural items related to southwest Virginia and its people. Contact: P.O. Box 742, Big Stone Gap, VA 24219, 703/523-1322.

THE HARRY W. MEADOR, JR. COAL MUSEUM — This museum owned by the Westmoreland Coal Company and operated by the Big Stone Gap Department of Parks and Recreation is located at E. Third Street and Shawnee Avenue. It is open to the public the year round and admission is free. This coal museum pieces together the treasure troves and memorabilia of private homes and public buildings from Big Stone Gap and surrounding towns. It tells the story of the past and tells how coal has influenced the local lifestyle. Contact: 703/523-4950.

NATURAL TUNNEL STATE PARK — Located in Clinchport, Virginia in Scott County. It is south of Big Stone Gap on US 23 some 17 miles. Called by William Jennings Bryan the "Eighth Wonder of the World." Natural Tunnel is believed to be one million years old. A very spectacular sight that has been missed by so many. It's a very different experience as evidenced by the following remarks in the folder put out by the Virginia Divison of Parks, "If you are near the tracks and hear a train coming, don't worry. Since the train will be moving slowly, you will have time to reach the pedestrian platform near the end of the 'little tunnel.' If you are in the Natural Tunnel when you hear a train there is plenty of room for both you and the train if you stay on the walkway." The Park has the following facilities: Swimming pool, Picnic, Hiking Trails, and a Visitor Center with displays and exhibits. Contact: Natural Tunnel State Park, Rte. 3, Box 250, Clinchport, VA 24244, 703/940-2674.

NORTH FORK OF POUND LAKE — Located in the Clinch Ranger District of the Jefferson National Forest is this primitive paradise. Camping, fishing, swimming, boating, picnicking. Contact: Clinch Ranger District, Rte. 1, Box 320-H, Wise, VA 24293, 703/328-2931.

FLAG ROCK — Located near Norton. This is a spectacular sight. Huge rocks with more breathtaking scenery. Camping and picnicking.

SPECIAL EVENTS — April—International Day Festival at Clinch Valley College; April or May—Lonesome Pine Arts & Crafts Festival; Memorial Day Weekend—Ralph Stanley Bluegrass Festival at Caney Ridge. 2nd Sunday, June—Tri-State Singing Convention in Big Stone Gap; 3rd or 4th week in August—Virginia-Kentucky District Fair.

For further information on this area contact: The Wise County Virginia Chamber of Commerce, P.O. Box 226, Norton, VA 24273, 703/679-0961 or 679-0965.

WYTHEVILLE
Lodgings: (703)
Econo-Travel Motor Hotel, E. Main St., Box 530, 228-5517
Holiday Inn of Wytheville, I-81, Ex. 23, 228-5483
Howard Johnson's Motor Lodge, I-81, Ex. 23, 228-3188
Johnson's Motel, US 11S, 228-4812
Wythe Motor Lodge, I-81, Ex. 23, 228-5525
Interstate Motor Lodge, I-81, Ex. 23, 228-8618

Campgrounds: (703)
Deer Trail Park, Rt. 1, Box 127B
High Bridge Camping Park, RFD 4
Wytheville KOA, Rt. 2, Box 118-B
Rural Retreat Lake Campground, RFD 1
Slopers Trout Farm & Campground, 686-4907
Stoney Fork Campground, Rt. 717W

Dining: (703)
Burger King, Lee-Hy Shopping Center, 228-8361
Durham's Restaurant, Main & 11th St., 228-5241
Fox Mountain Inn, I-81, Ex. 27, 637-3129
Hardee's, Main St., 228-7292
Holiday Inn-Southern Squire Restaurant, US 11N, 228-5483
Howard Johnson's, US 11N, 228-2425
Kentucky Fried Chicken, 1910 E. Main St.,
Log House Restaurant, 520 E. Main St., 228-5488

— Marissa J. Burton

Blue Ridge Market Days sponsored by Ferrum College's Blue Ridge Institute

FOX MOUNTAIN INN

Route 1, Box 492 (Exit 27—I-81—Graham Forge Exit)
Max Meadows, Virginia 24360
703-637-3129

Nestled in the rolling foothills of Southwestern Virginia — with Color
Cable T.V., H.B.O., E.S.P.N., D.D. Phones — Air Conditioned beau-
tiful Rooms —Shopping — Gas — Peaceful — Quiet — Tranquil
Setting.

Hosts: Curtis, Carnella, Carla Hopkins

Long John Silver's Seafood Shoppe, Wythe Shopping Plaza,
228-8481

McDonald's, 1195 N. Fourth, 228-5714

Pen-Bob Restaurant, Chapman Rd., 228-2266

Pizza Hut, 225 W. Lee Hwy., 228-3751

Western Steer Family Steakhouse, I-77 & Pepper's Ferry Rd.,
228-7103

Wilderness Road Truck Stop, Pepper's Ferry Rd., 228-8676

Potpourri

Wytheville dates back to 1839 and currently has a population of
about 7500. Wythe County was formed in 1790 and has a population
of about 24,500 people. The region is considered to be in the southwest part of the state. Elevation here is 2350 feet. Nearby Bland
County was formed in 1861 and has a population of 5550 people.
Elevation here runs between 2000 to 4000 feet.

Chief industries for the area are agriculture, mining, and manufacturing. The leading industry is agriculture. This region is one of the
leading livestock producing areas of the state and is the mainstay of
the farm economy.

The highway system places this region in a very favorable strategic
situation with I-81 and I-77 intersecting. There is US 11, US 52, US
21 to supplement the motor vehicular needs for the area.

Commercial air service is 70 miles distant from Bristol or 80 miles distant from Roanoke. Greyhound supplies frequent bus service and the Norfolk & Southern takes care of the railroad requirements.

The region is often referred to as the Mountain Empire. Within its confines is Wytheville Community College, part of the state's community college system. Radford University is 40 miles away while Virginia Tech is about 50. Emory & Henry is 50 distant in another direction while Bluefield College is no more than 35 miles distant.

Seventy-eight percent of Bland County is wooded. So very much of this untouched mountainous land is part of the Jefferson National Forest. There is little argument that this is one of the state's most beautiful and untouched parts.

The pioneer heritage that made this county great is exemplified by sturdy German and Scotch-Irish stock dating back to 1745. It has been the story of hardship and suffering. Fort Chiswell, in those pre-Colonial days was so vital to the early stability of the region. It was here during the French and Indian Wars that the military laid the foundation that the frontier's early development required.

It is interesting to trace the history of mining from the Revolutionary period. The ore from the lead mines was such that the mines have survived to this day. A shot tower was constructed on the banks of the New River which was important to the area's growth. It is a county landmark, to this day, and is one of either two or three in the nation. It was built in 1807 and was used to make lead shot for frontier settlers and Civil War soldiers.

The first resident physician for Wytheville was Dr. John Haller. In 1823 he bought and finished the "Rock House," a residence now owned by the Town of Wytheville. It is now the site of a museum and is a registered National Historic Landmark.

The area did not, because of remoteness, escape the Civil War. A local Wytheville heroine, not unlike Paul Revere, saved the community in 1863. Molly Tynes' exploits came about as the result of overhearing a plan in which the Union troops were to destory the railroad. At great personal danger she went through the untamed wilderness warning the citizens of the three contiguous counties of the approaching danger.

The area was again hit by attack the following year. It was repulsed so convincingly that the "Blueclads" turned tail to the mountains of West Virginia.

This is an area of hardy stock with people of warm and friendly disposition. The local inhabitants have always diligently cared for their land. To this very day they continue to preserve and enhance its ability to fruitfully provide.

Worthwhile Sights
BIG WALKER LOOKOUT — "Only the birds can see more," is the advertising theme that they use. Some 12 miles from Wytheville on US 52 is a scenic overlook as well as a swinging bridge, climbing tower, sky ride, hiking trails, picnic area, gift shop, and snack bar.

WYTHEVILLE NATIONAL FISH HATCHERY #2 — Twelve miles east of Wytheville may be found this hatchery which produces 150,000 pounds of rainbow trout annually. There is a five tank aquarium and other displays. Open to the public.

SHOT TOWER HISTORICAL PARK — Located at the point where US 52 crosses New River. It is some eight miles south of I-81 from Fort Chiswell off the I-77 Poplar Camp Exit. Open to the public Wednesday through Sunday; May through October. No charge.

HALE FISHING LAKE — Lake is stocked regularly with trout. It is located at top of Iron Mountain; south of Speedwell off US 21.

CARTER MEMORIAL WAYSIDE — Ten miles on US 11E. Picnic with good view.

Wytheville is located between Claytor Lake State Park in Pulaski and Hungry Mother State Park in Smyth County.

JEFFERSON NATIONAL FOREST — 51,000 acres are in Wythe County. Fishing streams, picnic areas. Investigate this for numerous outdoor activities. Horseback riding, hiking enthusiasts should consider. Forest available for hunting turkey, deer, bear, and small game.

CHAMBERS OF COMMERCE

Area Code 703
Unless otherwise indicated

Washington County Chamber of Commerce   628-8141
111 Russell Avenue
Abingdon, VA 24210

Bedford County Chamber of Commerce   586-9401
305 E. Main Street
Bedford, VA 24523

Greater Blacksburg Chamber of Commerce   552-4061
141 Jackson Street
Blacksburg, VA 24060

Christiansburg-Montgomery County
   Chamber of Commerce   382-4251
P.O. Box 418
Christiansburg, VA 24073

Radford City Chamber of Commerce   639-5037
103 Third Avenue
Radford, VA 24141

Greater Bristol Chamber of Commerce   669-2202
P.O. Box 519
Bristol, VA 24203

Greater Alleghany Highlands Chamber of Commerce   962-2178
241 W. Main Street
Covington, VA 24426

Charlottesville & Albemarle County
   Chamber of Commerce   804-295-3141
P.O. Box 1564
Charlottesville, VA 22902

Greater Bluefield Chamber of Commerce   304-327-7184
P.O. Box 4098
Bluefield, W. VA 24701

Culpeper County Chamber of Commerce   825-8628
133 W. Davis Street
Culpeper, VA 22701

Front Royal-Warren County Chamber of Commerce   635-3185
P.O. Box 568
Front Royal, VA 22630

Galax-Carroll-Grayson Chamber of Commerce   236-2184
P.O. Box 1006
Galax, VA 24333

Buchanan County Chamber of Commerce 935-4147
P.O. Box 672
Grundy, VA 24614

Harrisonburg & Rockingham County
   Chamber of Commerce 434-3862
P.O. Box 1
Harrisonburg, VA 22801

Lexington Visitors Center 463-5375
107 E. Washington Street
Lexington, VA 24450

Page County Chamber of Commerce 743-3915
Main Street
Luray, VA 22835

Greater Lynchburg Chamber of Commerce 804-845-5966
2015 Memorial Avenue
Lynchburg, VA 24501

Smythe County Chamber of Commerce 783-3161
P.O. Box 940
Marion, VA 24354

Loudoun Museum/Visitors Center 777-6093
16 W. Loudoun Street
Leesburg, VA 22075

Orange County Chamber of Commerce 672-5216
105 Byrd Street
Orange, VA 22960

Roanoke Valley Convention & Visitors Bureau 344-5188
14 W. Kirk Avenue
Roanoke, VA 24011

Staunton & Augusta County Chamber of Commerce 886-2351
P.O. Box 389
Staunton, VA 24401

Richlands Area Chamber of Commerce 963-3385
2418 Second Street
Richlands, VA 24641

Winchester-Frederick County Chamber of Commerce 662-4118
2 N. Cameron Street
Winchester, VA 22601

Wise County Chamber of Commerce 679-0961
P.O. Box 226
Norton, VA 24272

Wytheville-Wythe-Bland Chamber of Commerce	228-3211

Wytheville-Wythe-Bland Chamber of Commerce   228-3211
P.O. Box 563
Wytheville, VA 24382

State of Virginia Chamber of Commerce   804-644-1607
611 E. Franklin Street
Richmond, VA 23219

Shenandoah Valley Travel Association   740-3132
P.O. Box 488
New Market, VA 22844

Virginia Division of Tourism   804-786-2051
202 N. Ninth Street, Suite 500
Richmond, VA 23219

Virginia Department of Highways & Transportation
1221 E. Broad Street
Richmond, VA 23219

FESTIVALS

January
Lexington: Stonewall Jackson's Birthday Celebration

March
Bristol: Valleydale 500, Bristol International Raceway
Monterey: Annual Highland County Maple Sugar Festival

April
Charlottesville: Dogwood Festival
Front Royal: Virginia Championship Canoe Races
Leesburg: Oatlands Point-to-Point Races
Norton: Lonesome Pine Arts & Crafts Festival
Roanoke: Annual Wildflower Pilgrimage
Statewide: Annual Historic Garden Week
Vinton: Vinton Folklife Festival

May
Cumberland Gap: Spring Folklife Festival
Harrisonburg: Virginia Poultry Festival
Homestead: Spring Frolic Festival
New Market: Annual Re-enactment of the Battle of New Market
Roanoke: Festival-on-the-River
Winchester: Shenandoah Apple Blossom Festival

June

Harper's Ferry: Mountain Heritage Arts & Crafts Festival
Luray: Shenandoah National Park Hoover Days
Mt. Solon: National Hall of Fame Jousting Tournament
Pulaski: Pulaski County Flea Market & Antique Show
Pulaski: Annual Fiddler's Convention
Roanoke: Festival Week

July

Middletown: Annual Shenandoah Valley Farm Craft Days, Belle
    Grove
New Market: 19th Century Craft Days
Roanoke: Miss Virginia Pageant
Staunton: Happy Birthday USA

August

Abingdon: Virginia Highland Arts & Crafts Festival
Charlottesville: Ash Lawn Summer Festival/Colonial Crafts
    Weekend
Galax: Annual Old Time Fiddler's Convention
Mt. Solon: Annual Natural Chimneys Jousting Tournament
Woodstock-Orkney Springs: Annual Shenandoah Valley Music
    Festival

September

Edinburg: Old Time Festival
Grundy: Tri-State Gospel Singing, Breaks Interstate Park
Harper's Ferry: Mountain Heritage Arts & Crafts Festival
Middletown: Draft Horse Days, Belle Grove
Winchester: Apple Harvest Arts & Crafts Festival

October

Abingdon: Burley Tobacco Festival
Aldie: Annual Fall Harvest Festival
Bristol: Southeastern Band Festival
Ferrum: Blue Ridge Folklife Festival
Front Royal: Festival of the Leaves
Monterey: Annual Highland County Fall Foliage Festival
Waterford: Waterford Homes Tour & Craft Exhibit
Waynesboro: Fall Foliage Festival

November

Charlottesville: Blessing of the Hounds
Charlottesville: Thanksgiving Hunt Weekend
Leesburg: Loudoun Hunt Hunter Trials

December

Charlottesville: Christmas in Charlottesville Festival
Lexington: Jackson House Victorian Candlelight Tours
Winchester: Historic Christmas Tours

HISTORIC HOMES

Region 1
Berryville: Rosemont
Culpeper: Salubria
Culpeper: Burgandine House
Culpeper: Little Fork Church
Culpeper: St. Stephen's Episcopal Church
Culpeper: Virginia Baptist Farm
Leesburg: Oak Hil
Leesburg: Morven Park
Leesburg: Oatlands Plantation
Middleburg: Rokeby
Middleburg: Aldie
Middleburg: Belmont
Middletown: Belle Grove
New Market: Bushong House
Winchester: Stonewall Jackson's Headquarters
Winchester: Sheridan's Headquarters
Winchester: Daniel Morgan Home
Winchester: Old Stone Presbyterian Church

Region 2
Barboursville: Gov. James Barbour Home
Charlottesville: Monticello
Charlottesville: Ash Lawn
Charlottesville: Castle Hill
Gordonsville: Montebello
Harrisonburg: Daniel Harrison House
Orange: St. Thomas Church
Orange: Woodley
Orange: Montpelier
Staunton: Pres. Woodrow Wilson's Birthplace
Walnut Grove: Cyrus McCormick Home
Waynesboro: Swannanoa

Region 3
Appomattox: Appomattox Court House
Appomattox: McLean House
Bedford: Poplar Forest
Bedford: Elks National Home
Lexington: Stonewall Jackson House
Lexington: Lee Chapel
Lynchburg: Point of Honor
Lynchburg: Miller-Claytor House
Steele's Tavern: McCormick's Birthplace

PARKS

Region 1
Front Royal: Skyland National Park
Loudoun County: Algonkian Region Park
Loudoun County: Red Rock Wilderness Overlook Park
Luray: Shenandoah National Park
Manassas: National Battlefield Park

Region 2
Stuarts Draft: Shenandoah Acres Resort
Waynesboro: George Washington National Forest
Waynesboro: Sherando Lake

Region 3
Appomattox: Appomattox Court House National Historical Park
Clifton Forge: Douthat State Park
Clifton Forge: Green Pastures
Clifton Forge: Lake Moomaw

Region 4
Roanoke: Mill Mountain Park
Salem: Lakeside Amusement Park

Region 5
Abingdon: Washington County Park
Abingdon: Mount Rogers National Recreation Area
Abingdon: Grayson Highlands State Park
Bristol: Cherokee National Park
Cumberland Gap: Cumberland Gap National Historical Park
Grundy: Breaks Interstate Park
Grundy: Laurel Lake
Marion: Hungry Mother State Park
Pulaski: Claytor Lake State Park
Smyth County: Mount Rogers National Recreation Area
Smyth County: Clinch Mountain Wildlife Management Area
Tazewell: Crab Orchard Museum & Pioneer Park
Wise County: Natural Tunnel State Park
Wytheville: Shot Tower Historical Park
Wytheville: Jefferson National Forest

Blue Ridge Mountain Vistas Highlight Seasonal Splendor

St. Mary's River, Augusta County